INSIGHT COMPACT GUIDE

JERSEY

Compact Guide: Jersey is the ultimate quick-reference guide to this, the largest of the Channel Islands. It tells you everything you need to know about the island's attractions, from miles of sandy beaches to prehistoric sites, from flora and fauna to forts and fortresses, from museums and manor houses to Gerald Durrell's zoo.

This is one of more than 133 Compact Guides, which combine the interests and enthusiasms of two of the world's best known information providers: Insight Guides, whose titles have set the standard for visual travel guides since 1970, and Discovery Channel, the world's premier source of nonfiction television programming.

Star Attractions

An instant reference to some of Jersey's top attractions to help you set your priorities.

St Helier p14

Maritime Museum p15

Elizabeth Castle p20

Jersey War Tunnels p22

St Aubin p26

Gorey p45

Hamptonne Country Life Museum p35

Jersey

ersey – Queen of the Channel

The French writer, Victor Hugo, who lived in exile in ersey and Guernsey for 18 years, described the Channel slands as *'Fragments of Europe dropped by France and icked up by England'*. Forming part of the Duchy of Normandy at the time of the Conquest in 1066, these lots in the shadow of France have been linked with the British Crown for more than 900 years. However, as self-governing islands and strongholds of ancient, semi-eudal laws, they are not truly British, nor are they French. English is now the accepted language, currency s pounds and pence, yet street and place names are French, the food has a French slant and the islands feel listinctly foreign. Tourists are drawn by this combination of French flavour and British lifestyle – not to mention the location which is sufficiently far south to guarantee more daily hours of sun than anywhere else in Britain.

Beachcombers

5

The zoo's priority is preservation

Jersey is also a prosperous offshore tax haven. British celebrities and others fleeing the Inland Revenue have set up home here, lured by the agreeable lifestyle and appealing scenery as well as beneficial tax laws. For the tourist there is plenty to see and do. The island offers castles, museums, flower centres, potteries, German Oc-cupation relics, watersports, boat trips and a celebrated zoo. But for most visitors it is the coastline which is the greatest allure. Jersey has 50 miles (80km) of shoreline, 20 miles (32km) of sandy beaches – and nowhere on the island lies more than 2½ miles (4km) from the sea. More-over, the coastal scenery is highly varied, from the tower-ing cliffs of the north, to the Atlantic rollers of the windswept west and the spacious unspoilt sands of the south.

Location and size

The most southerly of the British Isles, Jersey lies in the Gulf of St Malo, 100 miles (160km) from the south coast of Britain, but just 14 miles (22km) from France. On most days Normandy is visible from the east coast of the island. The largest of the Channel Is-lands, Jersey is 9 miles (14km) long, 5 miles (8km) wide and covers an area of 45 square miles (72 sq km). However, the 350 miles (560km) of roads, many of them narrow winding lanes, make the island feel much larger than it actually is.

Jersey has two dependencies, both of them offshore reefs: Les Minquiers, (commonly known as 'the Minkies'), 9 miles (14km) south of St Helier, and Les Ecréhous, 5 miles (8km) off the north-east coast. Neither are in-habited, but both have a customs depot and

UNITED KINGDOM

English Channel

Alderney

Guernsey Herm
Sark

CHANNEL
ISLANDS   Jersey

FRANCE

St Brelade's Bay
Summer sun

6

weekend huts. Ownership of the reefs has often been the subject of dispute between France and Britain, and the matter was taken to the International Court in the Hague in 1953. Although the court ruled in favour of Britain, there are still occasional attempts by French adventurers to take possession of the reefs.

Climate

Jersey has the highest average number of sunshine hours in the British Isles, although the summer temperatures are no higher than those in some parts of southern England. In the summer months the island has a daily average of eight hours of sunshine and an average maximum temperature of 68° F (20° C). As in the UK, there is always the risk of bad weather, but clouds are often quickly dispersed by the strong south-westerly winds. The best months to go are May to September, July and August being the hottest. The Atlantic sea temperatures are cool for swimming, averaging 62.8° F (17.1° C) in summer.

The island has one of the largest tidal movements in the world and the coastal landscape undergoes dramatic changes between high and low water. During spring tides Jersey's surface area increases from 45 to 63 square miles (72 to 100 sq km) and the vertical difference between high and low water can be as much as 40ft (12 metres). The extreme tidal movements ensure the beaches are regularly washed, but also bring strong currents around the coast.

Government

When William, Duke of Normandy, conquered England in 1066, the Channel Islands formed part of Normandy. When King John lost his Norman dominions to the French in 1204, the islanders had to choose either to stay with Normandy or remain loyal to the English crown. They chose the latter and were granted the right to retain their Norman laws and customs. Because the English monarch's authority over the islands stems historically from the role of Duke of Normandy, Jersey's royal toast is 'The Queen Our Duke'.

Rule Britannia

The island's constitutional relationship with the UK has been confirmed by successive royal charters, thus maintaining the island's independent judicial and parliamentary systems. Despite its loyalty to the British crown, Jersey is therefore not constitutionally part of the UK. Such is the island's independence that it even issues its own currency and it is effectively only in matters of foreign policy and defence that it is subordinate to the UK. The island is not part of the European Union, but when the UK joined in 1973, the Channel Islands managed to negotiate very favourable terms concerning the free movement of manufactured and agricultural goods.

The monarch's representative in Jersey is the Lieutenant-Governor, who is a member of the British Armed Forces and is responsible for defence and military affairs. Jersey's legislature, the Assembly of States (known as 'the States') is presided over by the Bailiff. Its voting members comprise 12 Senators, elected for a six-year term, 12 parish Constables, elected every three years by the parishes, and 29 deputies elected triennially by popular franchise on a constituency basis. The need for a more effective and efficient government led to proposals for reform in 2001. The states, currently managed by committees, are to change to a new ministerial government, with 10 departments replacing the existing 25 committees.

The Bailiff heads the judiciary, with a chief magistrate and 12 honorary judges known as jurats. The island still retains the ancient institution of a non-paid, non-uniformed police force. Headed by the Constable, the members include Centeniers, Vingteniers and Constable Officers. This honorary police force, which works in conjunction with the paid, uniformed force, enjoys considerable authority and to this day maintains the exclusive right to charge suspects.

The legal system still retains certain feudal rights, one of which is the curious *Clameur de Haro* used, albeit rarely, to protect private property. With a witness either side the offended civilian goes down on bended knee and cries out: *'Haro! Haro! Haro! à l'aide, mon prince, on me fait tort'*. 'Haro' derives from 'Ahrou', the name given to Rollo the Viking, first Duke of Normandy and creator of the law. The rest translates: 'to my aid, my prince, I am being wronged'. The accused must then stop the offence until the case is heard in a court of law. If the Clameur is used without justification, the claimant is taken to court and fined.

Jersey's coat of arms

7

Maintaining standards

Bouley Bay

Language

Until the 1960s French was still the official language of Jersey. Even today a few words of standard French are used by the court and legal professions. Prayers are said in French before States and court sittings and the parliament votes *pour* or *contre*. Not so long ago a Jerseyman would have spoken English, French and the ancient Jersey Norman *patois* known as Jèrriais.

The language virtually died out but enjoyed a revival during the German Occupation as a useful means of covert communication, and today it can very occasionally be heard used by elderly Jersiais (the people who speak it) at rural events such as the cattle or agricultural auctions. Jersey-French language groups are anxious to keep this historic language alive and the signs at the airport and harbour now wish visitors *'beinv'nue a Jèrri'*.

The English language was first introduced to Jersey in the 18th century, and is now spoken by all the islanders. Street names on the island still carry their French names, often very different from the English names they were later given, e.g. La Rue de Derrière (King Street), La Rue des Trois Pigeons (Hill Street) and La Rue Trousse Cotillon (Church Street, but in French 'Pick up your Petticoat Street'). Most of the place names on the island retain their French names, and pronounciation still gives rise to some confusion for English visitors. Ouaisné, for example, is pronounced *Waynay*, and St Ouen, *Saint Wan*.

Economy and environment

Agriculture has traditionally been the mainstay of the economy. The Jersey cow, symbol of the island, is famous for its rich, golden high-fat milk, and the 'Jersey Royal', exported to the UK, is unmatched among new potatoes. However, agriculture and horticulture have suffered as a result of fierce competition from Europe. Today it is finance which is the main pillar of the economy. The advantageous tax laws combined with the economic and political stability have led to Jersey's role as one of the leading off-shore finance centres.

Freedom from UK taxes has lured wealthy British people to set up home on Jersey, among them TV personality Alan Wicker, musician Gilbert O'Sullivan, golfer Ian Woosnam and best-selling author Jack Higgins. Potential newcomers to the island are very carefully vetted and less than 10 a year are allowed entry. However, with the new recommended reforms for the island, the number is likely to increase.

Tourism plays an important role in the economy, though cheap flights to Europe have taken away some of the holiday trade in recent years. To lure back summer visitors and cater for demands beyond those of the sun-and-spade

Traditional costume at the Hamptonne Country Life Museum

8

The local breed

rigade, the island has focused attention on heritage and the arts, outdoor activities, gastronomy and the environment. In 1997 Jersey was the first destination in the world to achieve the Green Globe destination award, Green Globe being an environmental programme for travel and tourism developed in 1994 at the Rio Earth Summit. The island boasts some of the cleanest waters in Europe, aided by its award-winning ultra-violet sewage treatment system. Green lanes, reducing the speed limit on some country lanes to 15 mph, have encouraged cyclists and pedestrians, and clearly marked cycle routes now cover 96 miles (155km) of coast and countryside. On the negative side, Jersey still has a major traffic problem, especially in St Helier; it also generates a phenomenal amount of rubbish and the spread of reclamation site wastelands is evidence that the island is not yet entirely committed to restraint and recycling.

Flora and fauna

Jersey's mild oceanic climate and varied habitats attract flora and fauna which are rare or non-existent in mainland Britain. Among these are the loose-flowered orchid, or Jersey orchid, the agile frog, the Jersey green lizard and the Glanville fritillary butterfly. The rarest of the birds and one that is fast disappearing is the tiny and elusive Dartford warbler, which inhabits the gorse-strewn heathlands.

The Jersey green lizard

Les Mieilles Conservation Area, stretching almost the full length of Jersey's west coast, is a haven for naturalists. Sand dunes, scrub, freshwater ponds, reed beds and the adjacent seashore provide a variety of habitats for plants, birds and marine life. Les Blanches Banques to the south is regarded as the fourth most important sand dune system in Europe, supporting countless species of plants. Of these, 17 are recorded in the British Red Data Book of endangered and vulnerable plants.

The reed beds and marshy surrounds of St Ouen's Pond to the north lure scores of migratory birds, including sedge warblers and bearded reedlings. This was the first nesting site in the British Isles for Cetti's warbler and the nest can be seen in the Jersey Museum in St Helier. Other prime areas for ornithologists are the low-lying south and southeast coast, where the vast expanse of mud, sand and rocky outcrops exposed at low tide provides a rich breeding ground for thousands of wintering waders, gulls and wildfowl. Plovers, redshank, turnstone, dunlin, bar-tailed godwits, curlew and oystercatchers can be seen on an incoming tide along the rocky shore. Along the north coast, shags breed on the steep cliffs, sharing their rocky ledges with fulmars; and a small colony of puffins returns each year to its cliffside burrows on the northwest coast. Early morning and evening are the best time to see the birds.

Jersey lilies

Wild ducks

c6,500BC Previously attached to the land mass of Europe, Jersey becomes an island.

4,850–2,850BC The Neolithic Period. Settlers plant crops, raise animals, create flint tools, stone axes, pottery and querns (hand-mills for grinding cereals). Megalithic tombs or dolmens are erected, of which La Hougue Bie (*see page 44*) is the finest example. Archaeological discoveries include teeth of Neanderthal man, flint tools and bones of woolly mammoths and rhinos at La Cotte de St Brelade.

2,250–600BC Bronze Age. Bronze is used for weapons, jewellery and other luxury items. Late Bronze Age finds include the spectacular gold torque, found in St Helier. This long ornament of twisted gold was probably wrapped around parts of the body as decoration.

600BC–AD350 Iron Age. Larger settlements develop on the island. The main archaeological finds are hoards of coins from the 1st century BC. These may have been buried as news came of Romans sweeping northwestwards through France.

56BC Channel Islands become part of Gaul, but there is little evidence of the Roman Occupation.

6th and 7th centuries AD Britons, fleeing from the Saxons, arrive in Jersey via Brittany and bring Christianity to the island. St Helier arrives in Jersey in the 6th century and founds a hermitage in a cave near what is now Elizabeth Castle. Martyred by pirates in 555, he becomes the patron saint of the island.

9th century Vikings arrive in their longboats and ravage the islands.

933 King Rollo's son, William Longsword, annexes the Cotentin peninsula and the Channel Islands to the Duchy of Normandy. Normans make their mark with their code of laws, the foundation of the Common Law of the Channel Islands, their language (Norman-French) and seafaring traditions. Feudalism is introduced.

1066 Battle of Hastings. William the Conqueror gains the English crown and the Channel Islands become part of the Anglo-Norman realm.

1204 King John loses Normandy to King Philip of France. Channel Islands remain loyal to the English sovereign.

1215 In return for their allegiance, King John grants the Channel Islands customs and privileges, tantamount to self-government, which have since been confirmed by every English monarch. France is now the enemy and for the next 650 years the island is frequently threatened by French raids.

1200–1450 Construction of Mont Orgueil (Gorey Castle) to defend Gorey and Grouville Bays against French attacks. The castle is the main fortress on the island until the construction of Elizabeth Castle in the late 16th century. In 1338 Bertrand du Guesclin, Constable of France, invades the island but Mont Orgueil withstands the siege.

1461–8 Mont Orgueil captured by the French during the Wars of the Roses. Jersey under French rule for seven years, until it is retaken by Edward IV of England.

1483 Agreement between Edward IV and Louis XI of France that the Channel Islands and surrounding waters should be regarded as neutral in the event of war. (Agreement abolished in 1689.)

1547 The Reformation comes to Jersey, resulting in the destruction of all church stained glass, statuary, fonts, small chapels and roadside crosses. In 1550 all church property is sold by the Royal Commissioners. French Protestants (Huguenots) flee from Normandy to Jersey. When Elizabeth I comes to the throne, Jersey adopts Calvinism.

1500–1600 Construction of Elizabeth Castle on the islet of St Helier. Sir Walter Raleigh, Governor of Jersey from 1600 to 1604, names it after Queen Elizabeth I.

1608 States Act passed prohibiting the lucrative knitting of socks by men, women and children during the harvest period to encourage more people to work on the land.

1642–47 In the English Civil War, Jersey supports the Royalists.

1649 Charles I is beheaded. Charles II, then Prince of Wales, who takes refuge in Jersey, is proclaimed king by Sir George Carteret, Governor of the island. He later takes refuge again in Jersey as exiled King of England. As a reward, he gives Smith's Island and some neighbouring islets off Virginia to Sir George Carteret with permission to settle. These are renamed New Jersey.

1651 Following Cromwell's defeat of the Royalists, Parliamentarians are sent from England to Jersey to put down the Royalist resistance. St Aubin's Fort and Mont Orgueil are taken, but Elizabeth Castle withstands a siege of seven weeks. Carteret surrenders after an enemy bomb blows up the arsenal.

Late 17th century Commerce thrives, merchant sailors and shipbuilders grow rich on codfishing in Newfoundland. Fine merchants' houses built in St Aubin.

1779–1835 Construction of 30 coastal towers for defence of the island from the French.

1781 Battle of Jersey. French attempt to take over the island, under the command of Baron de Rullecourt. The heroic Major Peirson leads the local militia to victory in the Battle of Jersey, which takes place in St Helier's Royal Square. Both Peirson and De Rullecourt are killed in action.

1787 John Wesley visits Jersey, inspiring the Methodist movement.

1789 French Revolution brings aristocratic refugees, fleeing from the Reign of Terror.

1806–14 In anticipation of an attack by France, construction starts on Fort Regent, St Helier.

1815 After the French defeat at Waterloo, attacks from the French cease and Fort Regent is never used to defend St Helier. Influx of British army officers to Jersey, retired on half-pension.

1830s Heyday of the oyster industry.

1846 Queen Victoria visits Jersey. Victoria College opened in 1852 as a memorial to her visit.

1870 The Jersey railway is opened. St Helier is linked to Grouville in 1873 and to St Aubin in 1884, extending to Corbière in 1899.

1880s Steam ships mark the start of the decline of Jersey's lucrative shipbuilding trade.

1936 The Jersey Railway forced to close because of competition from buses and a fire which destroys most of the rolling stock at St Aubin.

1937 Airport opens at St Peter.

1940 Channel Islands demilitarised. 10,000 evacuated from Jersey. On 28 June the Germans bomb St Helier and demand peaceful surrender on 1 July. German forces move into Jersey.

1940–45 The German Occupation. The island is heavily fortified, and foreign prisoners are brought to the island to build defences. Rationing is introduced and supplies of food, fuel and medicine decline, particularly after D-Day. In the last months of the Occupation the neutral Swedish vessel, the *SS Vega*, brings Red Cross food parcels and other essential provisions.

9 May 1945 Liberation of the Channel Islands by British forces. King George VI and Queen Elizabeth visit the islands the following month.

1946 Royal Jersey Militia is disbanded after 600 years of service.

1948 French ceases to be the official language of the States.

1973 Britain joins the European Community. Special terms are agreed for the Channel Islands.

1980s Offshore finance becomes the main source of States revenue.

1995 Celebration of the 50th anniversary of liberation from German forces in 1945.

January 2001 The Clothier Report recommends the separation of the powers of the executive, the legislature and the judiciary, a president or prime minister for Jersey, and other major reforms.

October 2001 The states approve the Clothier Report recommendation to introduce a council of ministers to replace the current committee system of government.

2004 Jersey celebrates 800 years of allegiance to the Crown.

Elizabeth Castle

Preceding pages: St Aubin

Liberation Sculpture

Route 1

St Helier

Liberation Square – Maritime Museum – Occupation Tapestry – Church of St Helier – Royal Square – Central Market and Fish Market – Jersey Museum – Elizabeth Castle *See map on page 16*

St Helier, the capital of Jersey and its only real town, is the seat of the island's government and administration. It is not a place of great elegance and most of the older buildings have been demolished; however, it is home to the two best museums on the island, an historic castle and a central square steeped in history. Although many of the streets are thronged with traffic, the main shopping throughfares, with large stores, boutiques and lively food markets, are pedestrianised. The walk takes you through the historic centre, then out of the centre along the Esplanade to Elizabeth Castle.

Start at **Liberation Square ❶**, which was opened by Prince Charles on 9 May 1995, the 50th anniversary of the Liberation of the island from German Occupation. It was here that huge crowds gathered to see the British fleet sailing in to release the islanders after five long years under German rule. The prominent ★ **Liberation Sculpture** enlivens an otherwise unremarkable square, surrounded by a hotchpotch of architecture. The bronze group of figures, clutching at the Union Jack represent, from left to right: a Jersey couple of sufficient years to have witnessed the Occupation, a liberator, a Jersey fisherman and a farmer with his wife and children. Overlooking the square on the north side the Pomme d'Or Hotel was the headquarters of the German navy during the Occupation. The tourist office on the square used to be the terminus of the Jersey Railway which served the south and east coasts and it was from the rear of this building that some 2,200 residents were deported to Germany in September 1942.

Up on Mont de la Ville, overlooking the town, the walls and bastions below the modern white dome survive from the original **Fort Regent**, built at enormous expense in 1806–14 against the threat of French invasion. Troops were stationed here for many years, but it was never actually used to defend the island. In 1958 the fort was sold back to the States for £14,500, the original price of the land, and the building was then converted into a huge leisure centre, complete with sports facilities, swimming pools, concert halls, exhibitions and entertainment. The mast, to the far left, is the last working signal station in the British Isles. Dating from 1708, it is now used to signal weather warnings, high tides, shipping movements and anniversaries. The latest addition is the orange pennant which goes up when the plane carrying the daily national newspapers has left London and is lowered to half mast when it lands. The Union Jack on the west bastion is lowered to half mast only when a monarch dies, though an exception was made on the death of Diana, Princess of Wales.

Welcome to Fort Regent

15

The Steam Clock

Boat building at the Maritime Museum

Across the busy A1 south of Liberation Square, and looking like something out of Disneyland, the world's largest **Steam Clock** is modelled on a 19th-century paddle steamer. Wait long enough and it will start to foam, whistle and chime. A more worthwhile development on the waterfront is the ★★★ **Maritime Museum 2** (daily 10am–5pm or 4pm in winter) housed in a restored warehouse on North Quay. The museum, which opened in 1997, explores every aspect of the island's links with the sea, bringing to life its former role as a seafaring state. The museum offers plenty of hands-on exhibits and other activities. Visitors can feel the pull of the currents and the power of the sea, build a boat and sail it in the wave tank, listen to legends of the sea and watch the routes around the world made by Jersey vessels. Within the same building and covered in the admission charge is the ★★ **Occupation Tapestry Gallery 3**. This excellent display comprises 12 separate tapestries depicting scenes from the Occupation. These historically accurate and carefully-worked scenes were created by the 12 Jersey parishes. The themes range from the Outbreak of War and Deportation to the Daily Life of Civilians, such as the school-room scene of a boy yawning in a German lesson.

Return to Liberation Square and, on the far side, cross the Esplanade. Take the road leading up from the Southampton Hotel and cross over Wharf Street. Half way

Church of St Helier

up Mulcaster Street, the Lamplighter pub is decorated with stuccowork depicting the figure of Britannia between two cherubs and a garland of fruit below. This was the work of Turnkey Giffard, a prison warden who entertained his inmates by showing them how to carve. Take the next turning left into Bond Street, where Regency and Victorian buildings retain some of their original features. On the right the ★ **Church of St Helier** ❹ is named after the 6th-century hermit who preached from a rock beside what is now Elizabeth Castle (*see page 20*). The gate at the far end of the railings formed part of a screen used to segregate male and female prisoners during services in the Debtors' Prison. The church was formerly the hub of town

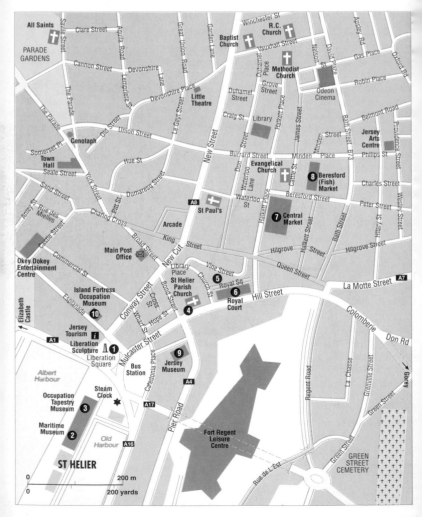

fe. Locals sought refuge here in times of crisis, elections were held here, bells were rung when enemy ships were sighted and orders were issued by the Constable. Major Peirson, hero of the Battle of Jersey (*see page 18*) is buried in the church, while Baron de Rullecourt, who led the enemy, has a small stone memorial in the graveyard.

Leave the church by the north side for Church Street. The name of the street looks somewhat prosaic beside the former French name of La Rue Trousse Cotillon or Pick Up Your Petticoat Street. This dates from a less salubrious era when ladies had to lift up their dresses to avoid the drains and sewers. Turning left into the street, note the house on the opposite side of the road (now the United Club), where John Wesley preached his gospel of Methodism in 1787. Further along on the corner is Jersey's first library, a Georgian building and one of the first on the island to be made of brick.

At the end of Library Place, to the left, the obelisk was erected in 1855 in recognition of Pierre le Sueur, who was responsible for the underground sewage system.

From Church Street turn into ★★★ **Royal Square** ⑤, formerly the marketplace, where proclamations were made, public executions took place, the occasional witch was burnt and criminals awaited trial in an iron cage. Today it is a peaceful square, shaded by horse-chestnut trees. The back of the United Club is the Registry Office, now used by UK couples taking advantage of a recent law which enables them to get married in Jersey. The building was formerly the corn market and inside original granite arches have been preserved. The 'V' for Victory which you can see marked in the paving in front of the building was secretly cut by a local stonemason who was re-laying the flagstones during the Occupation. Discovery of the act may well have led to deportation so he hid the 'V' under a layer of sand. The letters 'EGA' and '1945' were later added to commemorate the Swedish Red Cross vessel, *SS Vega*, which arrived towards the end of the Occupation with 750 tons of food parcels, relieving both occupiers and islanders from near-starvation.

Royal Square and insignia

The ostentatious **gilded statue** in the square depicts King George II (1727–60), dressed as Caesar, but wearing the Order of the Garter around his thigh. It was placed here and the square renamed when the King donated £200 towards the creation of St Helier's first harbour.

On the south side of Royal Square, the central building is the **Royal Court** (1866) ⑥, the island's court of justice, with the arms of George II above the entrance. It was from the balcony to the right that Alexander Coutanche, Bailiff of Jersey, hoisted the Union Jack on 8 May 1945 and relayed to the huge crowds Churchill's

The Peirson

Central Market display

Anthony Trollope's letterbox

message that the Channel Islands were to be liberated. To the east of the Royal Court is the States Chamber, whose Public Gallery, accessed on the far side from Halkett Place is open to visitors every other Tuesday when the States are in session. In the centre of the square a stone commemorates the dramatic Battle of Jersey that took place here in 1781. Baron de Rullecourt arrived secretly at La Rocque in the southeast corner of the island and led his small army to St Helier, before the islanders awoke. The Lieutenant Governor, still in bed, was tricked into believing that De Rullecourt had a much larger army, and surrendered. But a gallant young officer, Major Francis Peirson, ignored the surrender, rallied the troops, and after a brief but bloody battle, defeated the French in Royal Square. Both De Rullecourt and Peirson were mortally wounded and shot marks can still be seen on the building in the corner of the square which is now the Peirson pub. This was the last attempt by France to capture the island. Jersey's young hero was immortalized in John Singleton Copley's painting of *The Death of Major Peirson* at London's Tate Gallery, a copy of which hangs in the Royal Court.

Peirson Place beside the pub leads to **King Street**, a busy pedestrianised shopping thoroughfare. Opposite you Woolworths was formerly the grounds of the Governor's House. Turn right along King Street for Halkett Place named after a former Lt Governor of Jersey who served with distinction at the Battle of Waterloo.

Cross the street and turn left to get to the ★★ **Central Market** **7** (Mon–Sat 7.30am–5.30pm, except Thur 7.30am–1pm). This is a fine Victorian building with cast iron columns supporting the glass roof and an ornate circular fountain with cherubs, foliage and live goldfish. Market stalls were banned from Royal Square in 1800 and the new site chosen on the corner of Halkett Place and Beresford Street. The market erected here was pulled down and replaced by the new market in 1882. A favourite venue for both locals and tourists, this has 40 stalls selling fresh produce, flowers, Jersey lily bulbs, meat, cheese, bread and groceries. Outside the post office the hexagonal letterbox (1851) designed by the novelist Anthony Trollope, was one of the very first in the British Isles.

Leave the market at the Beresford Street exit and turn right. Across the road, the ★ **Fish Market** **8** has a fine selection of conger eel, bass, wrasse, grey mullet, shrimps, live lobsters, spider and chancre crabs and many other locally caught species. Head down here at 7.30pm to see the catch of the day arrive. At the far exit, turn left along Minden Place, cross Castle Street, and note on the right the Thesaurus Bookshop with an interesting choice of second-hand books.

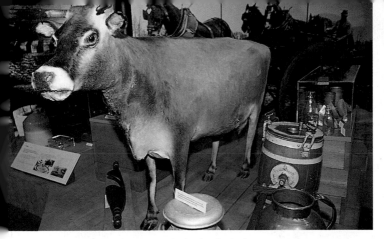

The award-winning Jersey Museum with dairy exhibits

Satyr at the Jersey Museum

At the next crossroads look to your right for the classical facade of the **Wesley Grove Methodist Church** (1847) at the top end of Halkett Place. John Wesley, who visited Jersey, Guernsey and Alderney, had a profound influence on the islanders and, by the 1820s, chapels, large and small, in the vernacular, Gothic or classical style were appearing all over the islands. This one used to seat 1,600. Methodism still has a strong influence on many of the islanders and several of the churches are still in use.

The prominent building with the pink, blue and russet stuccowork which you pass going up to the church, on the other side of the road, is the late Victorian Mechanics Institute. Originally called the Albert Hall, it's now a snooker club. Beyond it, the new library was opened by the Queen in 1989.

Make your way back along Halkett Place, to the far end of the street, passing en route the Evangelical Church, the market, and just before the end of the street on your right, the public entrance to the States Chamber, where the Order Paper for the day is normally posted. At the top, Hill Street, bristling with brass nameplates, is the street of advocates. Turn right into Mulcaster Street, then left for Pier Road. Just up the hill on the right is **La Société Jersiaise**, founded in 1873 for study and research into all matters relating to Jersey. The society runs an excellent library (Saturdays 10am–4.30pm) and maintains the neighbouring ★★★ **Jersey Museum** ❾ (daily 10am–5pm or 4pm in winter). This can be reached by taking the steps down to the courtyard and following the signs.

The museum, which has won major national awards, tells the story of Jersey from prehistoric to present times. Displays are highly informative and often enlivened by interactive videos and touch screens. Exhibits cover all aspects of the island including interesting sections on traditions and trades specific to Jersey, such as oyster catching, shipbuilding and knitting. The exhibition starts with a recreation of the Old Stone Age site of La Cotte de St Brelade (*see Culture, page 59*), showing the figures of Paleolithic man on the rockface and the bones of prehistoric woolly rhino found at the foot of the cave. Jersey was then part of the Continent and a display (on the first floor) shows how the sea level rose and the Channel Islands were formed. The second floor is devoted to works by Jersey artists, including 19th-century seascapes and landscapes and John Everett Millais' portrait of Jersey's most famous daughter Lillie Langtry. The top floor rooms, comprising school room and bedrooms, have been carefully reconstructed to show how they would have looked in Victorian times when the house was occupied by a doctor and his family.

For many visitors the favourite museum display is the Lillie Langtry memorabilia. Emile Charlotte Le Breton, as she then was, the daughter of a philandering Jersey dean, married a wealthy widower in 1874, and two years later took London society by storm with her beauty and charm. 'The Jersey Lily' became the mistress of the Prince of Wales, subsequently Edward VII, and later caused a further sensation by becoming the first society woman to take to the stage. The 'second Helen of Troy', as Oscar Wilde called her, died in Jersey and is buried in the graveyard of St Saviour's Church.

Occupation Museum (above) and Elizabeth Castle (below)

Exit the museum by the front entrance and look back at the facade. This handsome Georgian house, which once stood on the waterfront, belonged to a wealthy shipowner who contributed in 1820 to the cost of land reclamation and a harbour building scheme (now Commercial Buildings).

Return to your starting point, Liberation Square, to the west of the Jersey Museum and take the Esplanade for the **Island Fortress Occupation Museum** ⓾ (daily 9.30am–10.30pm). Housing one of several collections of German Occupation memorabilia on the island, this small museum features models of German soldiers, weaponry, documents and samples of the Red Cross food parcels. The story of the Occupation is covered on a video, with personal recollections of events by some of the islanders.

On the shore side to the west the huge new **Waterfront Centre** comprises housing developments, a leisure centre, night club, bars and fast food outlets. A large luxury hotel is in the pipeline. The project has provoked much debate among islanders for its utilitarian and stark architectural style.

No visit to St Helier is really complete without seeing ★★★ **Elizabeth Castle**, one of Jersey's major historic monuments (Apr–Oct, daily 10am–6pm, last admission

0m). Lying offshore from the Waterfront Centre (*see map, page 24–5*), this can be reached by the causeway leading to the islet in St Aubin's Bay where the castle stands. The causeway (about ¾ mile long) can be crossed on foot at low water, or there is the blue and white amphibian ferry (not included in the castle entrance fee) which travels at all tides.

Construction on the castle began in the late 16th century, by which time Mont Orgueil, built for bows and arrows (*see page 45*), was becoming increasingly vulnerable. Sir Walter Raleigh, the island's governor, who lived at the castle from 1600, called it Fort Isabella Bellissima (Elizabeth the most Beautiful), in tribute to his Queen, Elizabeth I. It was not until the 1640s when Jersey had been drawn into the English Civil War that the castle, which by now had grown considerably in size, came into its own. Charles II, then Prince of Wales, took refuge here, and did so again after the execution of his father, when Jersey proclaimed him King Charles II. During the war, Sir Philip Carteret, then Governor, sustained a siege here for 50 days and the castle was the last of Jersey's strongholds to surrender. Defeat came in December 1651 when a shell from from St Helier Hill (now Fort Regent) hit the abbey church and exploded the powder magazine.

The gun is fired at noon

21

The fortifications you see today date mainly from the 17th century, with the Guard House, hospital and workshops added in the early 19th century. The buildings around the Parade Ground house an exhibition covering the history of the castle, the museum café and the **Royal Jersey Militia Museum**, which has an exhibition of uniforms, medals and other military memorabilia. The Jersey Militia served the island for around 600 years and in their heyday numbered over 6,000 local men, divided into five regiments. To reinforce the military theme, Gunner Graves fires the noonday gun, and male visitors may be dragooned into marching the Parade Ground.

Hermitage Rock

The path behind the Militia Museum affords views over the breakwater to **Hermitage Rock**, home of the hermit who gave his name to the capital and parish. Son of a Belgian noble, he came to Jersey in the 6th century to devote his life to prayer, but was hacked to death by Saxon pirates in AD555. Legend has it that he picked up his head and carried on walking, much to the horror of the pirates. In the 12th century a small oratory was built over his cave and every year on the Sunday closest to July 16 a pilgrimage makes its way here, and a wreath is laid in his memory. For the best views of the coast, climb up to the gunnery control tower built by the Germans who modernised the castle with guns, bunkers and battlements.

Excursions from St Helier

Jersey War Tunnels

Jersey War Tunnels
Meadowbank, St Lawrence *See map, pages 24–5*

The Channel Islands were the only British territories to be invaded by German forces in World War II. Tiny possessions they may have been but Hitler saw them as the first step to his intended invasion of the United Kingdom. With remarkable speed, the islands were turned into impregnable fortresses. Thousands of forced, foreign labourers were used in the construction of defences around Jersey and today the bunkers, towers and gun emplacements stand out as stark reminders of those harrowing five years.

The most remarkable engineering feat of the Occupation is the ★★★ **Jersey War Tunnels** (formerly the German Underground Hospital; mid-Feb–mid-Dec 9.30am–5.30pm, last admission 4pm). From St Helier follow the signs to the west, and keep on the A1 by branching right at the end of the Esplanade. Keep on this inner road as far as Bel Royal, turn right on to the A11 and follow the signs for the hospital.

The massive network of tunnels and galleries, hewn from solid rock with gunpowder and handtools, was the work of thousands of forced labourers and Russian prisoners-of-war who toiled here in the harshest conditions. Creating the tunnels entailed the removal of 43,900 tonnes of rock and the cladding of 6,000 cubic metres of concrete.

The underground centre was originally designed as a bomb-proof artillery barracks, to protect the entire garrison of around 12,000 men against assault from sea or air. Sixteen tunnels were planned for the use of ammunition storage, armoured vehicles, fuel and food. However, the complex was never completed, for in the weeks leading to D-Day, with an Allied invasion looming, orders were given for the

Casualty ward

mplex to be turned into a casualty receiving station. Five ards were each designed to cope with 100 casualties. Unished tunnels were sealed off and the site was equipped ith operating theatre, recovery room, hospital wards, docs' and nurses' quarters, Officers' Mess, escape shaft, cenl heating, air conditioning and telephone exchange.

Officers' Mess

The anticipated invason never took place and the ccupying forces surrendered peacefully on 9 May 1945. he complex has gradually been restored as the most mprehensive museum of the German Occupation on the land. The hospital wards have been preserved or reconructed, and the the dark dripping tunnels have been aintained in their original, unfinished state. The xhibition, Captive Island, uses electronic digital techology to bring the Occupation years vividly to light. nstead of a ticket, visitors are given an identity card reting to an individual who features in the exhibition. Iany of these, including deportees, housewives and orced labourers, relate their experiences. The exhibits nclude a chillingly accurate reconstruction of the operting theatre, ready for the first casualty from an Allied nvasion that never happened. The recently created Garen of Reflection records details of those who died as a irect consequence of the occupation.

The Living Legend See map, pages 24–5

)pened in 1992 and billed as Jersey's number one ttraction, the **Living Legend** (Apr–Oct, daily 9.30am– .30pm; Mar–Nov, Sat–Wed only 10am–5pm) is an exensive purpose-built village offering a host of activities. rom St Helier take the A1 going westwards as far as 3el Royal, turn right on to the A11, then follow the signs.

Jersey Experience: recreating the past

Within the 9-acre (4-hectare) site is a craft and shoping village, landscaped gardens, street entertainment, restaurants, children's playground, two 18-hole adventure golf courses whose multi-level holes among aves, lakes and waterfulls present an amusing diverion for all ages. But what makes a visit here really worthwhile is the ★ **Jersey Experience** – a multi-sensory recreation of the history and traditions of the island. With ts dramatic special effects and lively dialogue, this is a firm favourite with children. Visitors start on the deck of a Victorian paddle steamer destined for St Helier, then, from a deck devoted to the island's millionaires, descend down the dark winding tunnel of time, encountering characters and creatures from local legends. Further down at 'the Island in the Sea', secrets are revealed of smugglers, shipwrecks and maritime myths. The auditorium is a mock-up of the Manoir de la Brequette, a manor house lost beneath the sea centuries ago. This is where the story of the island begins.

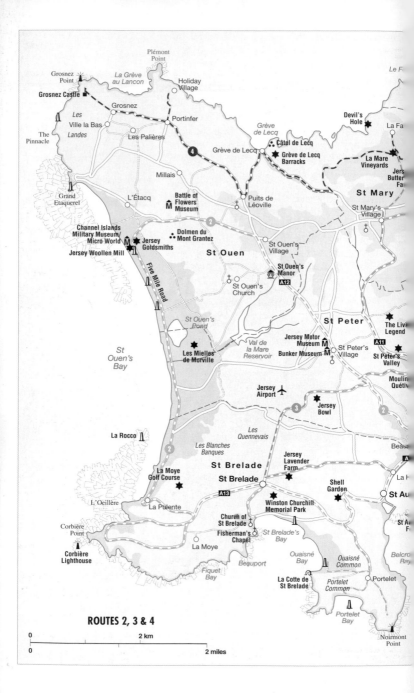

ROUTES 2, 3 & 4

0   2 km

0   2 miles

onez
Point

*St John's
Bay*

Fremont
Point

Belle Hougue
Point

Wolf's
Caves

*Bonne Nuit
Bay*

La Colombière

St John

133

Vicard Point

St John's
Village

Les Platons

Leicester
Battery

*Bouley
Bay*

A10

A9

Hautes
Croix

A8

Bouley
Bay

L'Etacquerel

La Hougue
Boëte

A9

*Jardin
d'Olivet*

ersey
lower
entre

Trinity
Village

*Handois
Reservoir*

Les Augrès
Manor

Carrefour
Selous

es

Hamptonne
Country Life
Museum

Trinity

St Martin

Pallot Heritage
Steam Museum

Jersey Zoo

St Lawrence

*Dannemarche
Reservoir*

Becquet
Vincent

Victoria
Village

St Lawrence's
Church

Waterworks
Valley

Augrès

Eric Young
Orchid
Foundation

German
Underground
Military Hospital

*Millbrook
Reservoir*

*Grands–
Vaux
Reservoir*

St Helier

St Saviour

La Hougue
Bie

A10

Five Oaks

La Hougue
Bie

11

el Royal

Millbrook

A8

A7

St Matthew's

A2

A1

St Saviour's
Church

A6

First
Tower

3

2

A9

Grouville

ST HELIER

4

A7

St Aubin's Bay

A1

The Waterfront
Centre

1

Grouville
Arsenal

Elizabeth
Castle

A4

Dicq

A5

Samarès
Manor

Mont Ubé

St Clements

Nicolle
Tower

*Grève
d'Azette
Bay*

St Clement

La Haguais

*St Clement's
Bay*

Continued from page 38

Continued on page 38

Torquay, Portsmouth, Poole,
ymouth, Guernsey, Alderney, Sark

St Malo, Granville

Green
Island

Maufant

Surf and Sand

St Aubin – Portelet Bay – St Brelade's Bay – Beauport – Corbière Lighthouse – St Ouen's Bay and Village
See map, pages 24–5

Occupation reminder at St Ouen's

The route takes in the best of Jersey's beaches, from the sheltered, sandy bays of the south to the dramatic west coast where surfers ride the big Atlantic swell. For most of the way the route follows the coast, revealing spectacular cliffs, quiet coves and, in the southwest corner of the island, the treacherous rocks around Corbière lighthouse, landmark of the island. The tour ends north of St Ouen's Bay, with a group of craft shops and a couple of small museums.

Leave St Helier via the Esplanade, following the signs for 'The West' and St Aubin, keeping to the coast all the way. The gently curving, south-facing St Aubin's Bay stretches for three miles between St Helier and the town of St Aubin. At the near end, Elizabeth Castle (*see Route 1, page 20*) stands on the rocks offshore. The seafront promenade, which used to be the Western Railway Line, stretches the length of the beach. During spring tides, giant waves crash over the wall here and sand bags can often be seen protecting the small streets leading up from the coastal road. At Bel Royal, where the A1 and A2 converge, keep to the coast road for St Aubin's Harbour.

★★ **St Aubin** is a smaller, prettier place than St Helier, well placed for walks along the coast, inland, or across the sands at low tide to the fort. Named after the Bishop of Angers, protector against pirates, the town ironically

St Aubin

acquired much of its wealth through profiteering and in the 17th and 18th centuries it was the main port on the island. During the English Civil War many a British vessel was captured and plundered by Sir George Carteret, the Royalist governor of the island. Such were the losses of British ships that parliamentary forces were sent by Cromwell to put down the Royalist resistance. Fortunes were also made by the more honourable trades of shipbuilding and codfishing in Newfoundland. Rich merchants built themselves fine four-storey houses, often equipped with huge cellars to store the booty. Some of the bulwarks stood on the seashore prior to the construction of the harbour and had spectacular roof outlooks for viewing the return of the fleet. One of the finest still standing is the **Old Court House**, overlooking the harbour, and now a hotel and restaurant. The loot was stored in the cellars and then divided in what was then the Court Room, presided over by the judges. The building had its moment of fame as the pub which featured strongly in *Bergerac,* the BBC Television cops and robbers series.

Al fresco at the Old Court House

At the end of the quayside stands the **Royal Channel Islands Yacht Club**, whose first female member was Lillie Langtry (*see page 20*). The strategically located **St Aubin's Fort** was built to command the western end of the bay in the mid-16th century. Persistent threats of invasion led to additional fortifications over the centuries, the most recent of which were built by the Germans during the Occupation. The fort, accessible only at low tide, is closed to the public. Before leaving St Aubin don't miss the pretty cobbled high street which rises steeply from the main road as it curves right. Known also as Rue du Crocquet, this used to be the main thoroughfare (for horses and carts) linking St Aubin with St Helier. The houses, many in local granite, were built by wealthy merchants at the end of the 17th century. The ones on your right would have backed directly on to the sea, enabling vessels to load and unload. On the left you will pass an art studio, antiques shop and café. Keep going to the top of the road for fine views across the bay.

Yacht Club insignia

Shell Garden

Turn inland from St Aubin along the A13, which climbs up the wooded valley towards St Brelade. On this steep road you are unlikely to miss the **Shell Garden** (Apr–Oct 9.45am–4.45pm), decorated with thousands of seashells. After ½ mile (1km) turn left at the corner shop along the Route de Noirmont and when you come to the small crossroads, take the left turn just beyond it for ★ **Noirmont Point**. This windswept headland, once known as Niger Mons or Black Hill, after the dark clouds which gather here, was acquired by the States of Jersey to commemorate the islanders who died in World War II. A prominent

Portelet Bay

relic of the Occupation is the huge underground Command Bunker of the former German coast artillery battery, complete with a large observation tower brooding on the clifftop. The bunker has been carefully restored by the Channel Islands German Occupation Society and is open to the public on Thursday evenings (7pm–9pm) and some Monday mornings (10am–noon). The Coastal Artillery gun to the left of it originally stood at La Coupe, on the northeast coast, but after the war it was thrown over the cliffs by the British, then recovered in 1979.

Return to the junction and turn left for ★★ **Portelet Bay**. Park the car at the top of the cliff, by the Portelet Inn, admire the views from the top of the cliff and/or walk down the long flight of steps to the delightful sheltered bay below. The little island, accessible at low tide, is properly called the Ile au Guerdain but more popularly known as Janvrin's Tomb, after the sea captain who was buried here. When Janvrin was returning with his ship from plague-infested Nantes in France in 1721, he was refused entry to St Aubin's harbour for fear of contamination. Janvrin fell victim himself and, since his body was was not allowed ashore, he was given a burial on the island. The body was later transferred to St Brelade's cemetery. The tower on the islet was built over the grave in 1808 as one of the many fortifications against possible invasion during the Napoleonic Wars.

From Portelet, return to the small crossroads, turn left and then take the right fork down to ★★ **Ouaisné Bay** (pronounced *Waynay*). The Smugglers' Inn, on the left as you go down, is evidence of former activities in this corner of the island. The magnicent sweep of beach, sheltered between headlands, stretches for over a mile, Ouaisné Bay being divided from St Brelade's by a rocky promontory called the Pointe le Grouin. Even on hot days in high season, Ouaisné's fine sandy beach has plenty of space.

At the southern end of the bay, a fissure in the cliffs marks a major archaeological site where teeth of Neanderthal man and the bones of prehistoric beasts were discovered (*see Culture, page 59*). Behind Ouaisné beach, the gorse-covered common is home to some rare species of fauna, including the Dartford warbler, the Jersey green lizard and the agile frog; but sightings are rare. The German anti-tank wall, stretching the length of the beach, was built by prisoners during the German Occupation. Portelet Common, an expanse of heathland above the beach, commanding splendid coastal views, can be reached by the cliff path that starts on the south side of the beach.

★★ **St Brelade's Bay** is accessible by foot either across the sands or over the rocky promontory, depending on

St Brelade's and Ouaisné Bay

Tea on the seafront

the tides. To reach the beach by car, return to the junction with the corner shop, turning left on to the A13, then fork left on to the B66 and descend to the bay. With its gently sloping, golden sands, sheltered setting and clear, blue waters, St Brelade's is justifiably the most popular beach on the island. Above the sands, the sea-front promenade is bordered by palm-lined gardens, cafés, hotels and gift shops. On the slopes above the bay lie some highly desirable tax-exile residences, surrounded by manicured gardens.

Fisherman's Chapel

At the western end of the bay, the picturesque ★★ **Church of St Brelade** sits on a rocky ledge, overlooking the little harbour. Built of pink granite boulders from the shore, the church dates back to the 12th century and still retains its Norman chancel. Step inside and switch on the lights to reveal the enchanting interior with its warm, granite walls and intimate atmosphere. Pebbles from the beach are embedded in the unrendered granite and the occasional limpet still clings to the roof.

Beside the church, the unique little ★★ **Fisherman's Chapel** is the oldest place of worship on the island, dating from the 11th–12th centuries, and built on the foundations of an older sanctuary. The chapel escaped destruction during the Reformation, and was variously used as an armoury, a store room for the sexton, a carpenter's shop and a meeting room. It was not until 1880 that permission was given for it to revert to a church. Restoration early in the 20th century brought to light the fragments of a series of beautiful medieval frescoes (1375–1425) decorating all four walls. These were restored in 1980 and today the scenes from the Old and New Testaments can be made out with the help of drawings on information boards which reconstruct the missing outlines. Clearest of all is the scene of the

Annunciation fresco

Church of St Brelade

La Corbière cliffs and lighthouse

Annunciation on the east wall. The small kneeling figures either side of the Virgin and Archangel – seven males to the left and seven females to the right – are members of the donor's family.

The flight of granite steps linking the churchyard with the small harbour is the shortest Perquage (sanctuary path) on the island. Before the Reformation, criminals who sought refuge in any of the parish churches were allowed to escape via such paths to the safety of a boat and sanctuary in France.

Take the steep road opposite the main entrance of the churchyard and then turn left for ★★ **Beauport**. This delightfully unspoilt bay is a favourite among islanders and smart yachts are often moored here on summer weekends. However, the climb down the hill and the absence of facilities on the beach deter most tourists, and it is seldom crowded during weekdays. If you are going to spend any time here – and it is a delightful place for swimming, snorkelling and sunbathing – take ample refreshments and a sunhat.

Leaving Beauport, turn left at the T-junction, and after ½ mile (1km) left again on to the B83 Route du Sud for ★★ **La Corbière**. Meaning haunt of the crow (*corbeau*), traditionally a bird of ill omen, this is a wild and desolate corner of the island, abounding in tales of shipwrecks. The first recorded disaster involved a Spanish vessel carrying a cargo of wine in 1495. Many other boats have foundered here, including the Royal Mail Steam Packet in 1859, with loss of life.

However, it was not until 1874 that a lighthouse, the first in the British Isles to be made of concrete, was built here. Perched on jagged rocks and surrounded by some of the roughest seas in the Channel, this makes a dramatic scene at any time of day. There are still occasional accidents here, the most recent involving a French catamaran, en route from Jersey to Sark, which struck a rock north of the lighthouse in 1995. The sculptured pair of clasped hands on the headland commemorates the rescue of all 307 passengers and crew.

At half tide you can cross the causeway to the lighthouse but the incoming sea is treacherous, so it is advisable to be aware of tide patterns. A carved stone on the causeway recalls the fate of an assistant lighthouse keeper who drowned while trying to save a visitor stranded by the incoming tide. Nowadays a siren warns visitors when the tide approaches the causeway. Originally manned by four keepers, the lighthouse today is automatic and there is no access inside for visitors. During the Occupation, the Germans built bunkers at Corbière and a massive observation tower to the east, now used by the local shipping radio.

St Ouen's Bay

For ★★ **St Ouen's Bay** to the north, continue around the headland, passing above the rocky Petit Port Bay, and in about a mile turn left on to the B35. The longest bay in the Channel Islands, the swathe of sands stretches in a great 4-mile (6-km) arc, all the way from La Pulente in the south to L'Etacq in the north. Throughout the year surfers make the most of the huge rollers on the incoming tides. Surf boards, boogy boards and wet suits can be hired at various points along the beach or, for those who prefer to sit and watch, the sea wall affords shelter and there are occasional cafés above the beach with seaview terraces (El Tico does the best food). All but experienced surfers should heed the danger warnings and keep to the areas between the flags where lifeguards are on duty during summer. La Pulente at the southern end is protected from the Atlantic swell and, if the tide is not high, there are sandy pools in the rocky outcrops which young children can enjoy.

31

La Rocco Tower

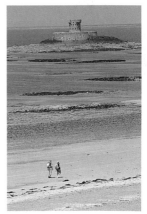

At the southern end of the bay **La Rocco** tower, dating from the turn of the 18th century, is the oldest of nine towers which were built to defend the bay during the Napoleonic Wars. Damaged by Germans target shooting during the Occupation, the tower underwent renovation in 1969. Only three of the other towers survive, one of them, **Kempt Tower**, being a fine example of a Martello tower (1834). This has been converted into a **Visitors' Centre** (May to September, Tuesday to Sunday 2–5pm) with informative displays on **Les Mielles Conservation Zone**. Exhibits cover landscape, ecology, history and prehistory, including information on the prehistoric relics among the sand dunes. The conservation area, which is the largest remaining area of unspoilt countryside on the island, is noted for its extensive sand dune system.

In autumn and winter tractors load up with *vraic* (pronounced 'rack') or seaweed from the beach for use as a

Traditional knitwear for sale

Life in a bunker at the Channel Islands Military Museum

fertiliser on the farmland bordering the coast. Horses and carts were once used for the job, gaining access to the beaches via slipways which you can see all the way around the Jersey coastline. In 1600 laws were passed to guarantee farmers equal rights to the free fertiliser. Today it is a free for all.

The beach is skirted by the confusingly named Five Mile Road – it is actually only 3 miles (4,5km) long. Follow this north, to the end of the main beach where the various tourist attractions of the Château Plaisir complex include the **Jersey Woollen Mills**, selling traditional Channel Island knitwear. Knitting is one of the islands' oldest traditions and records date back to the 16th century when women would knit sweaters to keep their menfolk warm on their long journeys to the cod banks in Newfoundland. Men knitted too and the manufacture of jerseys became so popular that in 1608, in order to encourage more workers onto the land, an act was passed prohibiting anyone over the age of 15 from knitting during harvest time. The penalty was imprisonment. Each jersey made on the Channel Islands had its own distinctive style and legend has it that if a sailor was lost at sea and his body washed ashore, he would be identified by his sweater and retuned to his native parish. The sweaters sold here are in fact made in Alderney with wool imported from the UK.

Close to the shore lies the ★ **Channel Islands Military Museum** (Easter to early October daily 10am–5pm), housed in a restored German bunker which once formed part of Hitler's Atlantic war defences. The museum is packed with Occupation memorabilia, British as well as German. Military and civilian exhibits include soldiers in uniform, military motorcycles, a rare Enigma decoding machine, Red Cross letters to relations and friends in England (limited to 25 words) and Christmas and birthday cards made by Jersey internees at Worzach and Bieberach camps in southern Germany.

Another tourist attraction of a rather different nature is **Jersey Pearl** over the road from the Château Plaisir complex. Here you can watch the pearl threading, have your own necklace made or choose from a range of cultured, freshwater or simulated pearls.

The main road heads inland after Jersey Pearl. The B35 takes you to L'Etacq, a vast expanse of reefs better suited to rockpool exploring than swimming. The old German bunker at the far end sells lobster, crabs, prawns and fresh fish. For a gourmet picnic, order lobster ready cooked (Faulkner Fisheries, tel: 01534 483500).

From L'Etacq you can continue up to Grosnez (*see Route 4, page 43*). The main road inland (B64) brings you the village of **St Ouen**. Behind the Parish Hall on the ar side of the A12, and marked off the road, is the **Bouchet Agateware Pottery** (daily 9am–5pm) where Tony Bouchet produces a wide range of pottery in the style of semi-precious stone (agateware). Although agateware has been produced in the past (and notably by ancient Chinese potters), Tony Bouchet's work is unique in its wide range of colours, and this is the only agateware pottery in existence today. The process, which has taken him decades to perfect, remains a closely guarded secret.

The **parish church of St Ouen's**, one of the finest on the island, lies southwest of the actual village, on the crest of a hill overlooking the sea. To get there take the C117 marked to the right of the A12. The church was mentioned in a charter signed by William the Conqueror prior to his conquest of England. Major alterations and extensions took place between the 12th and 19th centuries. The original building, possibly a chantry chapel built by 7th-century monks from Normandy, is thought to have been rebuilt or enlarged by a member of the historic de Carteret family, Seigneurs of St Ouen, whose nearby ancient seat can be seen from the main A12. The Manor of St Ouen (closed to the public), owned by the family for over 800 years, was used by Germans during the Occupation and St Anne's chapel was turned into a storeroom and butcher's shop.

The next village along the A12 is St Peter's, whose parish church has the tallest spire on the island and hence a warning red light for planes. A church has stood on this site for well over 1,000 years. Like St Ouen's, it predates the Conquest.

Return to St Helier by continuing south along the A12 and turning left on to the A1.

Fresh crab at L'Etacq

33

Helmets at the Military Museum

Lavender Farm: a blaze of colour

Tea at La Mare Vineyard

Route 3

Flowers and Farming

Waterworks Valley – Hamptonne Country Life Museum – La Mare Vineyards – Moulin de Quétive – Lavender Farm – Eric Young Orchid Foundation
See map, pages 24–5

Although agriculture is no longer a main source of income for Jersey, farming is still a way of life for the islanders. Over a third of the land is agricultural and the sunny south-facing slopes yield Jersey Royal potatoes and tomatoes, while the famous doe-eyed Jersey cow provides islanders with milk, cream and butter. Flowers are grown both for export worldwide and for the decoration of the floats at Jersey's celebrated Battle of Flowers *(see page 62)*. The island is also famous for its orchids, both wild and cultivated, as well as other species of rare wild flowers. This route takes you into the heart of rural Jersey to a Country Life Museum and a flower centre, followed by a vineyard, watermill and lavender farm and, finally, a detour to see some orchids.

From St Helier follow the signs for 'The West', taking you along the Esplanade. This becomes Victoria Avenue, venue of the annual Battle of Flowers which takes place every August and features bands, celebrities and a long parade of spectacular floats made of flowers. Apart from breaks during World War I and the German Occupation, the event has taken place every year since 1902 when the first 'Battle' celebrated the Coronation of King Edward VII. A day or two before the event volunteers can be seen busily cutting blooms and glueing them to the floats, though these days many are made of paper flowers. If you happen to miss the Battle, some of these amazing creations can be seen displayed around the parishes for a few days following the event.

When the road divides, follow the signs for the A1 which take you along the inner coastal road. Keep to this road until you see a turning to the right with a small sign for **Waterworks Valley** (C118). The stream along this peaceful, green valley used to power six watermills – hence the name of the road 'Le Chemin des Moulins.' The late 19th century saw the construction of the 3-mile (4.5km) long Millbrook reservoir, followed later by the Dannemarche and Handois reservoirs to the north, giving the valley its somewhat pedestrian name.

Beyond the Dannemarche Reservoir, where the road forks, turn left on to the C119 for the ★★ **Hamptonne Country Life Museum** (Apr–Oct, daily 10am–5pm; tel: 863955). This group of farmhouses and outbuildings in the heart of the countryside has been faithfully renovated to demonstrate 300 years of the island's rural heritage. The interiors of the two oldest houses have been recreated to illustrate living conditions of farming families in the 17th and 18th centuries. A third building is devoted to an informative exhibition demonstrating the changes in farming over the past 100 years and the decline in the island's agriculture – from 2,600 farms in the 1880s to just 500 today. At one end of the building the apple crusher and press are still used in the autumn to make cider. The restored outbuildings comprise stables, carriage house, bakehouse, wash house and farm labourers' accommodation.

This is very much a living museum with a *goodwyf* (*see page 8*) to tell you all the latest gossip from the 17th-century farming community or take you on a guided tour; there are also animals in the farmyard and demonstrations of bygone skills. The Hamptonne café makes home-made bread and cakes, as well as local specialities such as Jersey bean crock and Jersey Wonders. If you are here at lunch time, hampers can be ordered for picnics in the apple orchard. Ask at the café before you tour the site.

Descending the road from the museum turn right at the junction, then left and first right down a very narrow lane for the A10. Turn right and at the Carrefour Selous junction bear left on to the B39 for **Jersey Gold** (open all year 10am–5pm). Prices here are VAT-free and cheaper than those in the UK, but it is worth comparing them with the goldsmiths in St Helier before you make a purchase. You can watch the craftsmen at work, commission a piece of jewellery to be designed, see the Celebrity Memorabilia

Hamptonne Country Life Museum: cider press

Hamptonne guide

Exhibition or just relax in the gardens with ducks, swans and pink flamingos.

Continue along the B39 towards St Mary's village and then follow the signs to the Devil's Hole and ★ **La Mare Vineyards** (Easter to mid-Oct Mon–Sat). Centring around an old granite farmhouse, the vineyard comprises 12 acres (5 hectares) of vines, orchards and gardens. Visitors can wander freely around the estate, watch the audio-visual show describing the work of the vineyard, visit the distillery, cellars, and taste the white wines produced here. The vineyard shop also sells home-distilled Jersey Apple Brandy, as well as jams, jellies and mustards, all made at La Mare. Youngsters can be kept entertained by the miniature spotted ponies, Jersey calves and adventure playground. The Buttery Tea Garden tempts most visitors with home-made cakes, light meals and cream teas, made of course with the thick yellow cream from the Jersey cow.

Wine tasting at La Mare

Return to the main B33 in the direction of St Mary's Village and very shortly afterwards turn left on to the B26 signed to **St Peter's Valley**. This will join the A11 which runs through the valley. It was here that Queen Victoria was brought when she asked to see the most beautiful spot on the island. The valley was the site of six water mills, used mainly for grinding flour.

Turn right on to the B58, just over a mile along the A11, to see the only surviving mill on Jersey, the ★★ **Moulin de Quétivel** (Tues, Wed and Thur in season, 10am–4pm). A mill has operated here intermittently since feudal times, the current one dating from the 18th century. Abandoned in the early 20th century, it was revived by the Germans during the Occupation, only to fall into disrepair again. It was eventually brought back to working order by the National Trust in 1979. The top floor has an exhibition on the history of milling, while the first and ground floors demonstrate how the mill works. There is also an explanatory video which shows you how cabbage loaves (still sold in some bakeries on the island) are made in gorse ovens. The stoneground flour which is produced at the mill is sold in the ground-floor shop. An attractive footpath, through woodland, runs from the mill to the mill-pond.

LE MOULIN DE QUÉTIVEL
NATIONAL JERSEY 1936 TRUST
A mill with history

Continuing on the B58, go straight over the next crossroads for the A12. Turn left here and right at the roundabout which bypasses the airport and brings you into St Brelade. Just after the Quennevais shopping precinct turn left along the B25, signed to the ★ **Lavender Farm** (3rd week May to 3rd week September, Mon–Sat 10am–5pm). The fields of lavender, covering 9 acres

Harvest time at Lavender Farm

4 hectares), provide a blaze of colour throughout the summer. The *lavandage* or lavender harvest is usually over by mid-August but visitors can still watch the distilling and bottling processes and purchase oils and lotions made from the lavender essence. Further attractions are the herb garden, woodland walk and tea room.

To return to St Helier, continue along the B25 until you reach the coast road at St Aubin's. The A1 will bring you back into town. Alternatively you could end the route at St Ouen's Bay (easily reached from St Brelade via the A13 and B35), where some of the island's rarest species of flora are found (*see Route 2, page 31*).

Lavender Farm gardens

Detour to Eric Young Orchid Foundation

Floral enthusiasts should not leave Jersey without a visit to the ★ **Eric Young Orchid Foundation** (Wed–Sat only, 10am–4pm) northeast of St Helier. From the town take the ring road, following signs to 'The North', then turn off for the A8 to Trinity. After half a mile, turn right, following signposts for Les Grands Vaux and the Orchid Foundation. The road takes you alongside Les Grands Vaux reservoir, then to Victoria village where the Foundation is signposted to the left.

37

The late Eric Young devoted his life to breeding new hybrids of orchid and his exhibitions won prestigious awards. He first established a collection in Jersey in 1958 and within a decade it was recognised as one of the leading private collections in Europe. Young's ambition to set up an orchid foundation open to the public was achieved, but he died before the project was completed. The fruits of his lifelong efforts can be seen in the growing houses and the display area where orchids of dazzling colours are set against a backdrop of ponds, branches, rocks and raised beds.

Eric Young orchids

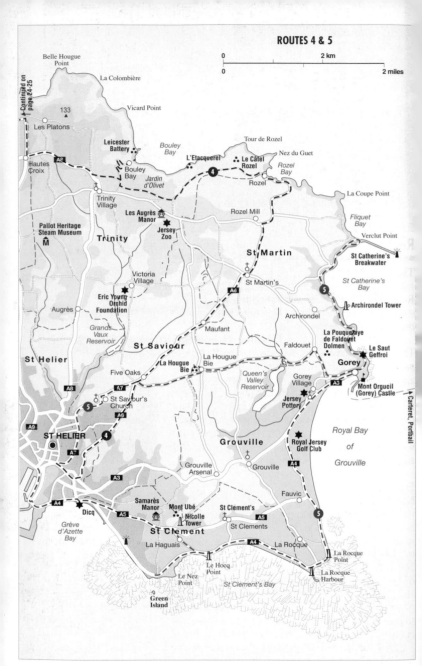

ROUTES 4 & 5

Continued on page 24-25

Belle Hougue Point

La Colombière

Vicard Point

133 ▲

Les Platons

A2

Hautes Croix

Leicester Battery

Bouley Bay

L'Etacquerel

Tour de Rozel

Le Câtel Rozel

Nez du Guet

4

Bouley Bay

Jardin d'Olivet

Rozel

Rozel Bay

La Coupe Point

Trinity Village

Rozel Mill

Fliquet Bay

Les Augrès Manor

Verclut Point

Pallot Heritage Steam Museum

Trinity

Jersey Zoo

St Martin

St Catherine's Breakwater

Victoria Village

St Martin's

St Catherine's Bay

Eric Young Orchid Foundation

A6

Archirondel Tower

Augrès

Archirondel

Grands Vaux Reservoir

Maufant

La Pouquelaye de Faldouet Dolmen

Le Saut Geffroi

St Helier

St Saviour

La Hougue Bie

La Hougue Bie

Faldouet

Gorey

Five Oaks

Queen's Valley Reservoir

Gorey Village

Mont Orgueil (Gorey) Castle

A8

A7

5

St Saviour's Church

A5

A3

Jersey Pottery

A9

ST HELIER

4

A7

Grouville Arsenal

Grouville

Royal Jersey Golf Club

Royal Bay of Grouville

→ Carteret, Portbail

A3

Grouville

A4

Samarès Manor

Mont Ubé

St Clement's

Fauvic

Dicq

A5

Nicolle Tower

St Clements

A5

St Clement

A4

La Rocque

5

A4

Grève d'Azette Bay

La Haguais

La Rocque Point

Le Hocq Point

La Rocque Harbour

Le Nez Point

St Clement's Bay

Green Island

0 ———— 2 km

0 ———— 2 miles

Route 4

Rozel Bay

The North Coast

Rozel Bay – Bouley Bay – Bonne Nuit – Devil's Hole – Grève de Lecq – Plémont – Grosnez Castle *See map opposite and on pages 24–5*

This glorious coast should ideally be covered on foot (*see page 52*), but it can also be admired from bays which are accessible by car. Alternatively, the bays can be used as a base for short sections of the 15-mile (24-km) north coast footpath. The route starts at Rozel Bay in the east, winds over the cliffs, dips down to sandy bays and ends at Grosnez Point at the northwesterly tip of the island. Allow a whole day for all the diversions, take a picnic lunch or stop at a simple café for freshly caught seafood.

Fishermen's huts and cafés

From the St Helier ring road follow the signs for 'The North' and the Five Oaks roundabout. From here take the A6 to St Martin's, then the B38 to ★ **Rozel Bay**. Tucked away in the northeast corner of the island, this is an unspoilt bay where fishermen's huts, cottages and cafés overlook the tiny harbour and the sand, shingle and rock beach. The pier was built in 1829 during the heyday of the oyster industry. Overlooking the bay, Le Beau Couperon Hotel was originally barracks, built in 1810 at the height of the Napoleonic threat. Being the closest point in Jersey to France, Rozel was considered a valuable defence site. However, no shot was ever fired here in battle.

Rozel Valley, reached by the road beside the Château La Chaire Hotel and Restaurant, makes a pleasant inland walk with its exotic trees and shrubs while the north coast cliff path (*see pages 52–3*) can be reached by taking the narrow lane up to the left of the Mimosa café.

Pleasure craft at Bouley Bay

Wild flowers above the bay

Cliffs at Bouley Bay

From Rozel return to the C93 and after 1½ miles (2km) turn right into Rue du Becquet. This joins the C95, and from here follow the signs for ★ **Bouley Bay**. As you near the coast the road snakes it way down through the wooded hillside to a pebble bay surrounded by high cliffs. The steeply shelving beach and the deepest waters around the island's shores are ideal for scuba diving. The **Jersey Diving Centre** based below the Water's Edge Hotel offers lessons and facilities to divers of all standards, including 'try dives' for beginners. Bouley Bay is also the venue of the highly popular spring and summer Hill Climbs, which take place up the steep road from the bay. Any member of the British Hill Climbing Assocation equipped with motorbike, saloon car, racing car, sports car or even a bike is welcome to participate. The village is otherwise peaceful, with no more to it than the hotel, a café above the beach and the **Black Dog** pub, named after the notorious Black Dog of Bouley Bay (*see page 62*).

On the east of the bay, perched above the sea and blending with the cliffs, the disused fort of **L'Etacquerel** was one of several defences built to guard the north coast from French invasions. Another was the **Leicester Battery** to the west, reached up the steps to the left just before the jetty. Cliff paths either side of Bouley Bay provide delightful walks. In summer the hills are ablaze with heather and wild flowers, while shags, which nest in cliff crevices in the spring, can be seen flying close to the shore.

Leaving Bouley Bay, climb back up to the top of the hill and turn right at the T-junction along the Rue de la Petite Falaise to join the main A8. Take the next main right turn (B63) and follow the signs for Bonne Nuit. To the right **Les Platons**, at 420ft (140m) above sea level, is the highest spot in Jersey – hence the forest of TV and radio masts.

The name ★ **Bonne Nuit** (Good Night) appears to have derived from the now non-existent Chapel of Bona Nochte, built in the 12th century. Conversely, the sea beyond the bay used to be called Maurepos (Bad Repose), possibly on account of smugglers. Today it is a secluded little bay, with a tiny harbour and a sand and shingle beach, sheltered below heather-clad hills. At low tide fishing boats and pleasure cruisers are beached on the sands, and resident ducks waddle across the bay, hoping for a crust from the Bonne Nuit beach café. The red wooden huts on the jetty belong to fishermen who go out daily for lobsters, crabs and clams and a notice on the small building near the café details the minimum size of each type of shellfish that can be taken out of the sea. In ancient times fishermen and other islanders rowed around Le Cheval Guillaume or Cheval Roc, the offshore rock, to protect them from evil spirits. Bonne Nuit pier is the finishing point for the Sark to Jersey Rowing Race, held every July, and a plaque, unveiled by Chay Blyth (who, with John Ridgeway, rowed the Atlantic in 92 days in 1966) commemorates the silver jubilee. The fastest rowers from Sark take about 2½ hours.

Ducks at Bonne Nuit Bay

On the promontory to the east of the bay La Crête Fort, built by the British in 1835, is the holiday retreat of the Lieutenant-Governor of the island.

From Bonne Nuit climb up the hill marked 'La Saline' (the C99), take the first lane on the right and, at the T-junction, turn right again for **Wolf's Caves**. The flight of steps to the right of the restaurant/bar will take you down 400ft (130m) to the 350ft (115m) long cave but it is only worth doing this at low tide. Ask at the bar for tide times and bear in mind that, as there are 307 steps, the climb back up is hard work.

Wolf's Caves

Returning along the access road to Wolf's Caves, take the first right turn down the very narrow Rue ès Nonnes to meet the C100. Known as La Route du Nord, this was built by islanders during the German Occupation. As you head northwest you will see a sign to Sorel Point, the most northerly point in Jersey, commanding splendid views to the west. East of the headland Ronez Quarry is one of the very few blots on the northern coastline.

The main road now veers away from the coast and becomes a green lane. At the next crossroads turn right for Le Creux du Vis (Screw Hole) or, as it is more popularly known, ★ **Devil's Hole**. Park at the Priory Inn and take the steep footpath down the hill to see the yawning chasm in the cliff, created by the erosion of the roof of a former cave. Most visitors keep at a safe distance behind a concrete wall well above the hole, others scramble down to sea level and watch the waters crash through as the tide comes up. The melodramatic name was acquired in

The devil at Devil's Hole

Grève de Lecq

Cell at the Barracks

Moulin de Lecq

the 19th century and probably derives from the figurehead of a mid-19th-century French shipwreck, which was found here and crafted into a wooden horned devil. Over the years various replicas of the devil have been placed on the path down, but each one has been stolen. The latest one towers over the pond at the start of the path near the pub, awaiting permission to be relocated at the hole.

Going south from Devil's Hole, take the second road on the right, past La Mare Vineyards (*see Route 3, page 36*). At the fork keep to the right for La Rue des Tourettes and turn left at the next fork for ★ **Grève de Lecq**. This very narrow one-way lane, dropping steeply to the bay, is a section of the north coast cliff path which veers inland to avoid the rifle range. Beware, therefore, of pedestrians. Sheltered by cliffs, with a sandy beach and rock pools, Grève de Lecq is the most popular bay on the north coast.

Behind the bay the **Barracks** (Tues–Sat 11am–5pm, Sun 2–5pm in summer) were built to house part of the British army garrison from 1810 to the 1920s. The buildings, restored by the National Trust, include the North Coast Visitors Centre, devoted to the wildlife and history of the area. The exhibitions provide detailed panels on the north coast footpaths, scenes from military life in the barracks, displays on Grève de Lecq's past and a collection of horse-drawn carriages.

Further up the main road, the **Moulin de Lecq**, which has been turned into an inn, was formerly a water mill. The stream here, which gushes out on to the beach, is the dividing line betweeen the parishes of St Mary and St Ouen. The massive mill wheel, which provides a dramatic backdrop to the Moulin de Lecq bar, is still in working order, though it is no longer used for grinding.

Overlooking the bay to the east and reached along the coastal path, **Le Catel de Lecq** is believed to be the site of an Iron Age hill Fort. At the east end of the bay you can make your way via the deep **Venus' Pool** to the long dark tunnel through the rocks to the otherwise inaccessible beach of Le Catel de Lecq. This is an exciting trip to a very secret beach but one that can only be done at low tide, preferably with a local to show you the way.

The last beach on the north coast is ★ **Plémont**, or more correctly La Grève au Lançon (Sand-eel beach). To get there take the road uphill out of Grève de Lecq, turning right on to the B55, and right again at the small crossroads at Portinfer, signed to Plémont Candlecraft. Plémont beach to the north remains unspoilt thanks to the lack of vehicular access. Leave the car at the park above the bay and walk down the path and steps. Low tide reveals a wide expanse of fine sands, rock pools and a network of caves in the liffs on the landward side; but at high tide the sea completely covers the beach. From the headland to the east, accessible by the North Coast footpath, you can sometimes see small numbers of puffins, razorbill and fulmars during the summer months. This northwest corner of the island feels quite remote, apart from the unsightly Holiday Village which sits on the headland.

Returning to Portinfer, rejoin the B55 for ★★ **Grosnez** (signed off the road), whose medieval castle ruins stand evocatively 200ft (60m) above the sea. The only recognisable feature is the Gothic arch, although the foundations of walls and buildings beyond it are clearly visible. A reconstruction on the information panel shows how the castle would have originally looked, complete with drawbridge, portcullis and machiolated upper storey. Nothing is known of the castle's history other than it was built in the 14th century and destroyed, probably by the French, either in the same century, or when they occupied Jersey in 1461–68. Carved corbels which once decorated the arch but fell off long ago can be seen in Archaeological Museum at La Hougue Bie (*see Route 5, page 44*).

Grosnez Castle

43

   Walk through the arch for fine views, weather permitting, of all the other Channel Islands. From left to right these are Guernsey, Jethou, Herm, Sark, and in the very far distance, Alderney. France lies in the distance to the east, while offshore, a chain of rocks known as **Pater Noster** (Our Father) is visible at low tide. The name originated from a shipwreck here, involving families who were on their way to colonise the then uninhabited island of Sark. Several of them were drowned, including women and children. Since then it has been customary for sailors and fishermen to recite the Lord's Prayer when passing the treacherous reef.

Ruins with a view

La Hougue Bie: the chamber

Route 5

Sights and Beaches of the East

St Saviour's Church – La Hougue Bie – Mont Orgueil Castle – St Catherine's Bay – Jersey Pottery – Samarès Manor *See map on page 38*

The route focuses on the the main sights in the east of the island: a prehistoric burial mound, a medieval castle and a manor house with atttractions for all ages. Beaches north and south of the village of Gorey provide a pleasant break from sightseeing.

Lillie Langtry at St Saviour's

Take the St Helier ring road, following signs first for the north and then for the A7 to the Five Oaks Roundabout. This will take you through the parish of St Saviour's, where Lillie Langtry (*see page 20*) was born. She was married twice in the **Church of St Saviour**, and is buried close to a beech tree in the churchyard. South of the church, Government House is the official residence of the Lieutenant-Governor, the Queen's representative on the island.

The mound at La Hougue Bie

At the Five Oaks Roundabout, turn right on to Princes Tower Road (the B28), passing the Esso garage on your left. At the next T-junction turn left for ★★ **La Hougue Bie** (Easter–Oct, daily 10am–5pm). This remarkable site, in the heart of the countryside, is dominated by a 40-ft (13-m) burial mound, covering a Neolithic ritual site, dating to about 3,500BC. The word 'Hougue' derives from the Norse *haugre* meaning a burial mound and the 'Bie' may be a corruption of the Norman family name of Hambye. One of the many legends surrounding the mound concerns the valiant Seigneur de Hambye who was called from France to slay the dragon of St Lawrence which was wreaking havoc amongst the islanders. He succeeded in his mission, but his squire, who had designs on the Seigneur's wife, murdered his master, and informed her that the dragon had mortally wounded her husband and that he himself was responsible for killing the creature. The seigneur's dying wish, he told her, was for his wife to marry the servant who had avenged his death. She agreed to marry the squire but the now Lord Hambye disclosed his guilt in his sleep. On discovering the truth Lady Hambye came to Jersey and buried her husband under a mound (La Hougue Bie), huge enough for her to see from the castle keep of Hambye (in Normandy).

Excavations under the mound in 1924 revealed a low passage leading to chambers made of huge stone blocks. Fragments of bone from eight bodies, flint tools, bones of sheep, pig and ox, beads, pottery and limpet shells were all discovered within the dolmen.

Neolithic axe

The pagan site was christianised by the construction of two medieval chapels on top of the mound. The oldest is Notre Dame de la Clarté, dating from the 12th century, but heavily restored. The Jerusalem Chapel, which preserves the faint outlines of two archangels, was built in 1520 by Dean Mabon who, according to puritanical sections of the church, made money by performing fake miracles in the church crypt. In the late 18th century the chapel ruins were transformed by the D'Auvergne family into a Neo-Gothic folly with a castellated wall and two towers. The Tour d'Auvergne, or Prince's Tower as it was known, was abandoned at the end of the 18th century but in the following century became a tourist attraction, offering panoramic views, a bowling alley and the Princes Tower Hotel.

Within the grounds of La Hougue Bie a museum of geology and archaeology displays some of the oldest rocks on the island and the bones and teeth of prehistoric animals discovered at La Cotte de St Brelade (*see Culture, page 59*). A legacy of more recent history is the German command bunker, displaying armaments and reconstructions of wartime sleeping and office quarters. The Germans also constructed a watchtower on top of the mound at the west end and 70 trenches within the grounds.

Turn right out of La Hougue Bie and follow the signs for ★ **Gorey** on the east coast. Nearing the village a steep road brings you down to that most famous of Jersey landmarks, ★★★ **Mont Orgueil Castle** (daily 9.30am–5pm, or dusk in winter). Translated as Mount Pride, and also known as Gorey Castle or Le Vieux Château, this mighty fortress towers over the harbour and commands the entire east coast. It is an impressive site at any time of day, but particularly picturesque after dark in summer when the

45

battlements are floodlit. The castle was built on the orders of King John, after he had lost Normandy and the Channel Islands had decided to remain loyal to the British crown. During its long history, this impregnable fortress rarely succumbed to the successive attacks from the French. The notable exception was an invasion in 1461 when the fortress fell into the hands of the French for seven years. With the construction of Elizabeth Castle, designed to meet the demands of modern-day warfare, Mont Orgueil became redundant; and were it not for the intervention of Sir Walter Raleigh, who thought it a shame to lose such a 'stately fort', it would have been razed to the ground. In the 17th and 18th centuries the castle played various roles: a stronghold of the Royalists in the English Civil War, a state prison under Cromwell, a refuge for French aristocrats and the headquarters of a spy network during the French Revolution. A fine example of a concentric castle, Mont Orgueil was sited on an Iron Age hill fort and designed with a series of independent defences, with walls going straight out of the rock.

Gorey by night and day

A climb up the steep battlements to the 13th-century keep will be rewarded by stunning views. In the medieval rooms at the top, where the Governor and his staff lived, a series of tableaux depict events from the rich and turbulent history of this medieval fortification in Tudor times. The restoration of the **Tudor Great Hall**, a project which has given rise to much controversy, is due for completion in 2004. A series of tableaux with taped commentaries illustrate episodes from the castle's roles as 16th-century fortress, 17th-century political prison and 18th-century spy base. Among the prisoners was William Prynne, the 17th-century puritan who was branded a seditious libeller (hence the initials 'SL' engraved on his cheek); another tableau illustrates three Royalist prisoners who unsuccessfully tried to escape the castle by knotting sheets together.

At the top of the castle the 16th-century **Somerset Tower**, adapted by the Germans as an observation post, commands superb views. France can usually be seen across the water and on a really clear day you can make out the power station at Cap de la Hague on the tip of the Cherbourg peninsula.

In the shadow of the castle lies the quaint harbour of **Gorey**, where shops, pubs and cafés cluster around the waterfront. The village developed in the early 19th century when the flourishing oyster industry gave Gorey the sobriquet of 'the pearl of the east'. In 1820 English fishing fleets invaded the coast to share in the profits but by the middle of the century the oyster beds had been over-dredged and the industry was all but over. Today the harbour protects a fleet of pleasure craft and, as the only official seaport in Jersey apart from St Helier, offers high-speed catamaran trips to the Norman ports of Carteret and Port Bail (*see page 73*).

The coast road north of Gorey, the B29, climbs up towards the rocky promontory known as Le Saut Geoffroi or **Jeffrey's Leap**, named after a convicted criminal and renowned womaniser who managed to survive unscathed after his punishment of jumping from the cliffs to the rocks below. He was declared a freed man but, eager to impress the fair sex, he decided to perform the feat again. This time, however, his luck ran out.

Just beyond Jeffrey's Leap Café, a narrow lane on the other side of the road leads up to ★ **La Pouquelaye de Faldouet**, a Neolithic dolmen (*see Culture, page 59*).

The main road skirts the pebble and sandy bay of Anne Port, and follows the coast by the bay of Havre de Fer and past the distinctive red and white **Archirondel Tower**, built in 1874. Keep to the B29 for **St Catherine's Bay**, enclosed to the north by a ½-mile (1-km) long breakwater which was built as a result of a British blunder in the mid-19th century.

Archirondel Tower

In answer to a naval base at Cherbourg and other French coastal installations, the British Government chose this site (as well as one at Alderney) for a harbour. Despite warnings that the depth of water was insufficient and the harbour would silt up, the project nevertheless went ahead and breakwaters were built here and at Archirondel. Twenty years and £250,000 (sterling) later, the project was abandoned. The St Catherine's arm of the harbour was preserved and a lighthouse built at the end.

Today the breakwater is popular for fishing and promenading. The coast road stops here, but you can get to Fliquet Bay to the north on foot.

Lobster pots at St Catherine's Bay

The road going south from Gorey Harbour and skirting the Royal Bay of Grouville (*see below*) brings you to Gorey Village, where the chief attraction for tourists is the ★ **Jersey Pottery** (Mon–Sat 9am–5.30pm all year, but no pottery production on Saturday). This is a highly organised commercial enterprise, where visitors can watch at close hand all the processes of pottery production, from the raw clay stage to the decoration and glazing. At each stage there are information boards with clear explanations of the techniques used. Tours end at the show room displaying a large range of ceramic tableware and decorative pieces, including Jersey-themed pieces such as the bean crock, milking can and Jersey cow.

The Garden Restaurant

Gourmets come to the pottery for food alone. The *à la carte* Garden Restaurant, with a Michelin award for high-quality cuisine at affordable prices, has the reputation for some of the best seafood on the island. A cheaper, less formal alternative is the neighbouring nautically-themed Spinnaker Grill.

Continuing south, to the east of the main road lies the ★ **Royal Bay of Grouville**, which stretches for 3 miles (5km) between Gorey and La Rocque Point. Guarding the bay are a number of towers built as coastal defences in the second half of the 18th century. These fortifications were armed and manned, but never actually used to defend the island. Queen Victoria, so impressed by this long and spacious sandy bay, gave it the Royal prefix after her visit in 1859. Shortly on the left are the links of the **Royal Jersey Golf Club**, the most exclusive on the island.

The route returns to St Helier via the coast road (A3 and A4), stopping at the little harbour of **La Rocque** in the southeastern corner of the island. It was here that Baron de Rullecourt and his troops secretly landed in January

Royal Bay of Grouville

1781, en route to their defeat at Royal Square in St Helier (*see Route 1, page 17*). Low tide reveals a huge expanse of reefs and gullies, and Seymour Tower, standing on a rocky islet 2 miles (3km) to the southeast, can be reached on foot. Beware, however, of the large tidal flow and the rapid incoming waters.

From La Rocque continue on the A4, detouring briefly after 2½ miles (4km) at **Green Island**, a small rocky outcrop covered in grass (hence the name), accessible by foot if the tide is not too high. Prehistoric graves, along with human and animal bones, were discovered here in 1911, but were removed for safekeeping to the Jersey Museum. The island has been gradually eroded by the sea and restorers are currently trying to prevent it from being washed away. On the waterfront the Green Island Restaurant is one of the best places on the island for freshly caught fish and seafood.

49

Japanese garden at Samarès Manor

Directly north, off the A5, lies ★★ **Samarès Manor** (Easter to early Oct, daily 10am–5pm). The highlight of the parish of St Clement, the manor house has 14 acres (5.7 hectares) of beautifully landscaped gardens, incorporating a Japanese garden, ponds with swans and ducks, an ancient dovecot and a delightful walled garden full of culinary, cosmetic and medicinal herbs.

The manor house, which is still a private home, can be visited on a guided tour, Mon–Sat mornings. The name derives from the Old Norman French *Salse Marais,* or salt water marsh, dating from ancient times when the owners profited from the saltpans on the lowlying land to the south. Farmyard animals, horse-drawn rides, falconry demonstrations and parrot shows provide plenty of entertainment for children. Craft displays include the Jersey Woodturners who make walking sticks out of the famous Jersey Giant Cabbage. Otherwise known as Cow Cabbage, Jersey Kale or Long Jacks, the six-foot tall cabbages were grown all over the island in the 19th century. Used for *soupe à choix*, boiled with potatoes and lard, they also served as cross rafters, bean poles, cow fodder, fuel and for the well-known Jersey cabbage loaf.

Woodturning display

St Clement's best-known resident was Victor Hugo, who lived here for three years after his exile from France. In 1855 he was expelled from Jersey for his support of newspaper articles discrediting Queen Victoria for making a state visit to Paris. The next 15 years of his life were spent on Guernsey. A plaque on the side of a large rock at **Le Dicq** slipway commemorates the spot where Hugo delivered orations to his fellow exiles. Le Dicq, situated south of Howard Davis Park in St Helier, can be reached by taking the coastal route (A4) back to the capital.

One of the famous lowland gorillas

Jersey Zoo

Les Augrès Manor, Trinity (tel: 01534 860000)
Open daily except Christmas Day, 9.30am–6pm or dusk

Feathered friends

Gerald Durrell and his wife, Lee

Headquarters of the Durrell Wildlife Conservation Trust, the ★★★ **Zoo** was founded by author and naturalist Gerald Durrell in 1963 and today is internationally renowned as a sanctuary and breeding centre for some of the world's most endangered species. This is no ordinary zoo. 'The idea behind my zoo was to aid in the preservation of animal life,' Durrell wrote, 'to build up under controlled conditions breeding stocks… so that, should the worst happen and the species become extinct in the wild state, you have, at least, not lost it forever. Moreover, you have a breeding stock from which you can glean the surpus animals and reintroduce them into their original homes at some future date.' At Durrell's memorial service in 1995, Sir David Attenborough spoke of the zoo's priorities, which entailed putting 'the animals first, the staff second and the public as privileged paying guests'.

Breeding programmes have been developed with the Trust working in close cooperation with the governments and trainees of the native countries of the endangered species. More than 300 trainees from 70 different countries have studied at the International Training Centre for the Captive Breeding and Conservation of Endangered Species, started up with funds raised by the Trust's US sister organisation and opened in 1984 by the Trust's patron, the Princess Royal. Many of the animals are the last survivors of their species and the zoo is their only chance of survival. The Trust continues to fulfil Durrell's ambition to reintroduce animals bred in captivity to their native habitat.

Among the success stories are the pink pigeons bred in Jersey and reintroduced to the forests of Mauritius, the golden lion tamarins which have been released in a private reserve in Brazil, and the thick-billed parrots, considered extinct in Arizona, which are now flying free in their native pinewoods. One of the recent releases was a pair of St Lucia parrots who flew courtesy of British Airways back to the Caribbean, accompanied by the Prime Minister of St Lucia who travelled to Jersey especially to escort them home.

The audio-visual presentation, 'Before Another Song Ends', interpreting the work of the Trust, provides an entertaining and informative introduction to the zoo.

Twenty-five acres (10 hectares) of parkland and watergardens, with rare flowers, shrubs and trees, are the setting for this exotic collection of mammals, birds and reptiles. Throughout the zoological park the Trust has tried, wherever possible, to cultivate the native habitat of the animals' wildlife. Compared to most zoos, the enclosures are spacious and imaginative, providing natural environments for family groups of endangered species.

Golden-headed lion tamarin and endangered reptile

Favourite inmates are the Sumatran orang-utans who provide endless entertainment in their splendid habitat of islands and waterways, the rare reptiles from Round Island, Mauritius, the marmosets and tamarins living free in the woodlands, the Livingstone fruit bats, with a wingspan of 6ft (almost 2m) and – most famous of all – the lowland gorillas. Beside the compound a statue commemorates Jambo, the mighty gorilla who hit the headlines in 1986 when he protected a 5-year-old boy who fell into the enclosure. The 'gentle giant', who fathered 13 offspring, was the first male gorilla to be reared in captivity.

Jambo

A moated enclosure near the entrance is home to a family of ring-tailed coatis and a much-loved and long-established pair of Andean bears, Wolfgang and Barbara. The only bears in South America, the Andean species until recently faced threat from farmers who blamed the bears for damaging their crops. Nowadays the chief hazard comes from Asian hunters who hunt the bears for their livers which yield bile to which superstition ascribes a medicinal use. A glass-domed interpretation centre, semi-submerged into the landscape, gives access to the enclosure and provides a 'behind-the-scenes' opportunity to demonstrate the role and techniques of breeding endangered species. The development also features a bronze sculpture of Gerald Durrell with a lemur and gecko; it was made by the celebrated sculptor John Doubleday. The latest addition to the zoo is the Cloud Forest which recreates the scents and sounds of a South American rainforest.

Drama along the north coast

LA VALLETTE WALK

From bay to bay

Walking on Jersey

To experience the beauty of rural Jersey and the undeveloped stretches of coastline, there is no better way than to walk. The island may be small, but it offers some surprisingly dramatic and varied scenery, particularly along the northern coastline. The rural interior offers walks through woodlands, along valleys, reservoirs and through leafy lanes with granite farms and cottages. In addition to the official footpaths there are 45 miles (72km) of Green Lanes, where the speed limit is a sedate 15 mph, giving priority to pedestrians and cyclists. These roads are well signed with a special logo at the beginning and end of each lane. Other roads on the island tend to be busy in season and are best avoided by walkers. The network of footpaths continues to grow as the States open up new stretches, both along the coast and inland, often in conjunction with the Jersey National Trust and other landowners.

Jersey Tourism produces a short, cheap guide featuring five walks on the island. A map available from the tourist office marks footpaths; alternatively, there is the more detailed Ordnance Survey 1:25,000 map of Jersey, which marks every footpath, boundary and building. When exploring the coast, visitors should watch out for extreme tidal movement, one of the largest recorded in the world. During the third and fourth hours of a rising spring tide, the rate of rise can be as much as 2½ inches (5cm) a minute. Tide tables are available from shops, and are also posted in the *Jersey Evening News*.

North coast

The north coast footpath offers mile after mile of majestic cliffs and dramatic rugged scenery. This is easily the most exhilarating walk on the island and one that can either e done in its entirety over a very long day, or preferably n separate sections at a gentler pace. The walk can be done t any time of year, but the scenery is at its best in spring when sea campion, thrift, ox-eye daisies, pennywort and bluebells are in full bloom. This is also the time of year when you might spot the Glanville fritillary butterfly dancng over the cliffs. Before undertaking the walk it is worth aying a visit to the North Coast Visitor Centre at the Barracks at Grève de Lecq. Maps and leaflets showing the footpath network are available and illustrated panels show you what to look out for en route.

Feeding time

The official footpath, a good deal of which was constructed by Jersey prisoners in the 1980s, runs almost the entire length of the north coast, all the way from Rozel in the northeast to Grosnez in the northwest (you can actually start at the headland at La Coupe in the far northeast, but the going is tricky between here and Rozel). The path occasionally breaks from the coast, diverting through wooded slopes or fields, and in St John's Parish, it joins the main road following the coast before heading inland to avoid the only two blots on the north coast seascape: the rubbish dump at La Saline and the unsightly quarry at Ronez. Most of the time the route is well signed but a map is neverthless useful. The whole walk is 15 miles (24km) long and it can be done by taking No 3 bus from St Helier to Rozel (the path begins behind the village) and No 8 back from Grosnez.

Grosnez Point

For those who want to do a section at a time, there are various points along the coast which are accessible by car or bus. Perhaps the most spectacular stretch is Bouley Bay (No 4 bus from St Helier) to Bonne Nuit (No. 4 bus). Timetables are available from the bus station at the Weighbridge in St. Helier – they are also published in some of the free holiday publications. Parts of the walk are quite steep, particularly as the path climbs up from the bays, but there is nothing which would really challenge an averagely fit adult. Benches at regular intervals enable you to rest and admire the views, there are also cafés and pubs at the small fishing harbours en route. The views are stunning all the way, and at the eastern end you can see across to France. In the west the walk ends at the ruins of Grosnez castle, which stand above black sheer cliffs and command views to the north of the other Channel Islands.

One section at a time

For stopping points along the coast, such as the fishing harbours, Wolf's Caves and Devil's Hole, *see Route 4, page 39*, which covers the north coast by car.

West coast

Although it lacks the exciting cliff scenery of the north coast, the footpath skirting the wild and windswept St Ouen's Bay offers a bracing walk. Surfers provide plenty of entertainment and there are cafés along the way which make the most

Pond life

Corbière lighthouse

of the views. Conspicuous landmarks along the bay are the coastal defence towers: La Petite Tour or Lewis Tower, Kempt Tower (now a Visitor Centre) and the offshore La Rocco Tower to the south, all erected as defences against the French from 1778 to 1835. Behind the beach the sand dunes of Les Mielles Conservation Zone and the pond of St Ouen are a haven for naturalists (*see Route 2, page 31*). Leaflets on the flora and fauna of the area are available from the Visitors' Centre at Kempt Tower, and bird buffs can fill in a checklist of 72 birds to be seen in Les Mielles. Exploration in the sand dunes here will also reveal Neolithic menhirs and the relics of more recent history in the foundations of 40 purpose-built huts which accommodated over 1,500 German prisoners during World War I. To the south of St Ouen's Bay, Corbière lighthouse can be reached by causeway if the tide is not high (*see Route 2, page 30*). This is a favourite place to watch the sea and the sunset.

North of St Ouen's Bay the windswept clifftops between L'Etacq and Grosnez provide splendid views along the coastline. This walk can be done either as an extension of the north coast footpath, or as a short 3-mile (5-km) walk starting either at Grosnez or L'Etacq. Along the way the five-storey observation tower is a prominent German landmark on the clifftop and a coastal artillery battery (open most Saturdays from May to mid-September) has been carefully restored with gun emplacements and bunkers.

Further south, the 200-ft (60-m) high menhir-like rock known as The Pinnacle was an ancient ceremonial site, occupied in turn by Neolithic, Bronze Age, Iron Age and Roman settlers. The common here, called Les Landes, is the largest area of heath on the island, renowned for its wild open spaces and spectacular sea views. Exposed to Atlantic winds, it nevertheless supports a rich variety of wild plants and is strewn with gorse and heather in summer. It is also home to Jersey's racecourse, a rifle range and an airfield for model aircraft.

The southwest

The delightful southwest coast can be covered on foot, starting at Ouaisné Bay and ending at La Corbière. If the tide is high St Brelade's Bay can be reached from Ouaisné over the rocky promontory dividing the two beaches. At the far end of St Brelade's Bay, beyond the church above the tiny harbour, a path leads to the idyllic beach of Beauport. To reach the bay, you have to climb down the stepped path from the clifftop. From Beauport there is a path, though not always a very obvious one, along the rugged coastline to La Corbière. The scenery en route is not enhanced by the prison, radar station and desalination plant but these at least are useful landmarks. The route is otherwise scenic, affording some splendid coastal views.

For shorter strolls, Portelet Common, on the headland between Portelet Bay and Ouaisné Bay, commands stunning views over Ouaisné and St Brelade's Bay to the northwest and over Portelet Bay to the east. Noirmont Promontory, visible beyond Portelet Bay, and accessible by car, is not quite as scenic but neverthless provides pleasant clifftop strolls and historic interest in its German Occupation relics (*see Route 2, page 27*).

East coast

This is not Jersey's most exciting coast, and there are relatively few paths that follow close to the seashore. One of the worthwhile sections is the walk from Gorey to St Catherine's. (Bus No 1 or Easylink 77 will take you from St Helier to Gorey Pier, No 20 will bring you back from St Catherine's Bay). The route provides good views of the coast and on the way you can stop at Jeffrey's Leap and the Pouquelaye de Faldouet dolmen (*see Route 5, page 47*) and Archirondel beach, which makes a good spot for a picnic. The path from here takes you to St Catherine's Breakwater, a popular spot for anglers and promenaders. Off the approach road to the breakwater, an upper and a lower footpath lead to the rocky Flicquet Bay, which marks the end of the coastal path.

From this northeastern corner of the island there are good views of Les Ecréhous, the reef of rocks lying midway between Jersey and Normandy. In the early 14th century a prior, monk and one servant lived on Maître Ile, the largest of the reefs, and the remains of a small chapel can still be seen here. Today the islets are popular with sailors from Jersey and France.

From Gorey you can also walk southwards along the promenade to Grouville Common. Watch out here for stray golf balls because the common is home to the Royal Jersey Golf Club. Further south, there are steps in the

Sanctuary path at St Brelade's

Noirmont Point

Royal Jersey Golf Club

sea wall which give access to the beach. At low tide you can walk right around the southeastern tip of the island via La Roque and Le Hocq, to Green Island.

Inland walks

The most scenic inland walks focus on valleys and reservoirs. The path alongside Waterworks Valley, running north from Millbrook, follows the winding road past reservoirs and through wooded slopes. To the west, the Jersey War Tunnels is a good starting point for walks through attractive woodland along St Peter's Valley. In the northeast of the island, there are delightful walks in the thickly wooded valley of Rozel Woods, between St Catherine's Bay and St Martin's village. The path circling the Y-shaped Val de la Mare reservoir is an easy 3-mile (4.5-km) walk providing fine views of the distant St Ouen's Bay from near the dam. Queen's Valley Reservoir, west of Gorey, provides another pleasant, undemanding walk which takes you around the trout-filled waters.

The railway walk

The now defunct Western Railway, linking St Helier with St Aubin, was extended to Corbière in 1884. Trains ran on a single line of standard-gauge track and, apart from delays caused by waves crashing over the sea wall along St Aubin's Bay, the service ran with remarkable efficiency. However, competition from buses and a fire at St Aubin's station led to the demise of the service in 1936. The track was turned into a footpath and today makes a delightful 4-mile (6-km) walk across the western corner of the island. The start of the path is signed off the main road as it turns inland from St Aubin's harbour. (Take bus Nos 12, 14, 15 or Easylink 55 to St Aubin.)

St Aubin

There is no need for a map here – just follow the path until the end of the line. Along the latter part of the walk, the trees took a heavy battering during the hurricane of 1987, but new ones have been planted. The railway line ended above Corbière, and the old station is now a private house. Corbière lighthouse can be reached along the causeway providing the tide is not too high. If you do not want to make the return journey on foot, the buses (*see above*) departing from the terminus will take you back to St Aubin or St Helier.

A wide range of escorted walks is organised by the Gerard Le Claire Environment Trust from May to September. The walks are for all ages and abilities and are escorted by experienced and knowledgeable guides. The majority of the routes are free of charge and prebooking is not required. Information is available from Jersey Tourism, St Helier or from the Kempt Tower Visitor Centre at St Ouen's Bay.

Cycling Tours

Along the green lanes

No distance on Jersey is too far to cycle and the network of quiet country lanes and coastal roads make for pleasant, if at times strenuous, cycling. Since the introduction of the Green Lane Scheme, cycling on the island has become much more popular. Cycle routes have been established all over the island and the clear signs along the way enable you to explore the winding lanes without constantly referring to maps. If a rural lane suddenly ceases to be a Green Lane, the probability is you have cycled across a parish boundary; three pro-car parishes are still resisting the Green Lane scheme. For visitors who want to plan their own cycling itineraries, Jersey Tourism publishes a very useful map, marking the coastal circuit, inland links and connections to various popular attractions. Jersey Tourism also publishes a first-class cycling guide with five very detailed routes, 15–18 miles (24–30km) in length. Refreshment stops are highlighted along the way.

57

Speed limit for cars

Jersey Tourism (tel: 01534 500777) offers guided cycle tours from the Visitor Services Centre on Sun and Wed during the season. The tours last three hours and cover the history and heritage as well as the natural beauty of the island. Prebooking is normally required.

The easiest introduction to a cycling holiday, particularly suitable for families with small children, is the designated footpath/cycle track following the old railway line above the bay from St Helier to St Aubin. The Railway Walk (*see facing page*) following the extension of the line to La Corbière, can also be used by cyclists.

Cyclists in St Helier

For cycle hire, see page 70. For escorted,guided bike tours contact Jersey Cycle Tours, 2 La Hougue Mauger, La Rue des Touettes, St Mary, JE3 3AF (tel: 01534 482898, fax: 484060). They operate Apr–Sept and provide free delivery and collection.

Antiquity

Ancient tree stumps, visible very occasionally at St Ouen's Bay when the sand has been washed away by storms, are relics of a submerged prehistoric forest which existed before Jersey became an island. Originally forming part of the land mass of Europe, it broke away in around 6500BC, the last of the Channel Islands to do so. Palaeolithic man set foot on the island well over 100,000 years ago to hunt game and shelter in caves which were then many miles inland from the sea. Conspicuous evidence of their occupation are the human teeth, flint chippings and bones of mammoth and woolly rhinoceros discovered at La Cotte de St Brelade cave on the south side of Ouaisné Bay.

The first discoveries were made in 1881 but excavations continued on and off for another hundred years, revealing invaluable information about successive Palaeolithic hunters who lived here. Today the cave is considered one of the most important Palaeolithic sites in Europe. The mounds of animal bones found at the foot of the 98-ft (32-m) cliff suggested a specialised hunting technique whereby herds of prehistoric animals were stampeded to their death over the cliff edge. The cave is closed to the public, but relics, including teeth of Neanderthal man and the bones of animals, are on view in the Jersey Museum, St Helier (*see Route 1, page 19–20*) and in the museum at La Hougue Bie (*see Route 5, page 45*).

59

Inside La Hougue Bie's chamber

Neolithic man, who arrived on the island over 6,000 years ago, left his mark in the monumental tombs and the standing stones which lie scattered around the island. The most impressive of the chambered tombs are the early passage graves or burial chambers, made of huge boulders and approached by a tunnel-like passage. These enigmatic monuments, often associated with fairies, played an important role in the rich folklore of the island. The most spectacular of these ancient sites is La Hougue Bie, a cruciform passage-grave whose huge mound was later crowned with two medieval chapels. La Pouquelaye de Faldouet, lying on a plateau inland from Gorey, is a long passage grave, badly damaged by diggers but nevertheless retaining an air of mysterious antiquity.

In 1785, during defence constructions on the hill now occupied by Fort Regent, an extensive dolmen was discovered resembling a mini Stonehenge. Since the grave was impeding construction of the fort, it was presented as a retirement present to General Conway, then Governor of the island. The mighty megaliths and capstones were shipped across the Channel and taken up the Thames to grace the general's private estate upstream from Henley-on-Thames, where the dolmen stands today.

The French wars

From 1204, when King John lost the English territories in France and the Channel Islands elected to remain loyal to the English crown, hostilities prevailed between the islands and France. Jersey was frequently threatened by invasions and fortifications were constructed, particularly along the vulnerable east coast, lying just 15 miles (24km) from Normandy. Mont Orgueil (Gorey Castle) was built overlooking Grouville Bay and remained the main stronghold on the island for nearly four centuries. This great medieval fortress withstood many attacks from the French, including a devastating raid in 1373 by the Constable of France, Bertrand du Guesclin, otherwise known as the Black Dog of Brittany. The castle fell just once in 1461, and a French force captured and held Jersey for the next seven years. By the end of the 16th century, Mont Orgueil could no longer withstand the attacks of modern warfare and Elizabeth Castle (*see Route 1, page 20*) was built on an islet in St Aubin's Bay.

Jersey's distinctive round towers (not to be confused with the later cam-shaped Martello towers) were built in the late 18th century as part of Governor Conway's plans to defend the coast against further possible invasion from the French. The lower storey served as a store for arms and provisions, the upper floor as accommodation for one officer and 10 men and the top of the tower as the gun platform. Towers and forts were built around the shoreline, particularly along the east and west coasts. The building programme was accelerated after the attempted French invasion in 1781 led by Baron de Rullecourt. The French were defeated at the Battle of Jersey, thanks to the gallant young Major Francis Peirson (*see page 18*). Seymour Tower, unique among Jersey's coastal towers for its square plan form, was built in 1782 off La Rocque Point, where

BATTLE OF JERSEY
JANUARY 6TH 1781
THE FRENCH TROOPS UNDER THE COMMAND
OF BARON DE RULLECOURT
CAME ASHORE HERE

Officer's room in Elizabeth Castle

de Rullecourt had landed. In all, 31 coastal towers were built on the island, of which 24 survive.

By the early 19th century, with the collapse of peace after the Treaty of Amiens, Napoleon railed against Jersey as 'a nest of brigands', forcing the governors to improve the island's defences and construct a fortress on the hill above St Helier. Fort Regent was built in 1814, but was never used to defend the town. The Battle of Jersey was thus the last attempt by the French to attack the island.

German Occupation

In June 1940, after the evacuation of Normandy, the British Government reluctantly withdrew their troops from the Channel Islands. Ten thousand islanders were evacuated to England. On 1 July German planes dropped an ultimatum, demanding unconditional surrender. The Occupation of the islands – the only part of the British Empire captured by Hitler – began the following day and was to last for five years. Jersey, like Guernsey, was turned into an impregnable fortress, with thousands of foreign labourers used to construct coastal bunkers, continuous anti-tank walls, observation towers and artillery batteries. These concrete structures were left standing after the war as historic relics. Most evocative of all the German fortifications is the Jersey War Tunnels (*see page 22*) where slave labourers toiled in harrowing conditions to complete a huge complex of bomb-proof artillery barracks which was never actually used.

German observation tower at Corbière

For the islanders times were hard with rations, medicines and domestic fuel in short supply, particularly in the latter stages of the Occupation. A curfew was imposed, land requistioned, private vehicles confiscated, the sale of spirits banned and, worst of all, radio sets were confiscated. The rationing gave rise to ingenious substitutes for everyday comestibles such as acorn coffee, pea pod tea and roseleaf tobacco. In 1942 more than 1,000 British-born islanders were deported to Germany, the majority for political activities or for harbouring forbidden radio sets.

Following D-Day in June 1944, the Germans were cut off from mainland France, fuel was running out, and both islanders and occupiers were on starvation rations. In December the Bailiff appealed to the Red Cross and at the end of the month, the Swedish ship *Vega* arrived with 750 tons of Red Cross parcels. Five months later, on 8 May 1945, the message from Churchill was broadcast in Royal Square: '…and our dear Channel Islands are also to be freed today'. Liberation Square in St Helier – the spot were jubilant crowds greeted the British liberators – was opened on the 50th anniversary of that memorable day. The Liberation Sculpture, dominating the square, commemorates the event.

Liberation Square

Folkore and Festivals

Folklore

Jersey abounds with myth, superstition and strange customs. Prehistoric menhirs and dolmens gave rise to devil worship and witchcraft, and stormy seas sowed the seeds of legend. Many are the tales of the wreckers who lured ships onto the treacherous reef of Corbière by burning fires near the rocks, indicating a a safe haven from the stormy waters. The inevitable shipwreck would bring death to the crew and precious cargo to the fishermen. In medieval times the Seigneur of St Ouen was entitled to any booty washed ashore near his manor and there are records showing that in 1495 a cargo of wine from a Spanish shipwreck was plundered by the seigneur with the aid of parishioners. On the north coast tales were told of the Black Dog of Bouley Bay, a terrifying creature with huge saucer eyes that roamed the coastline of the bay. The dog in fact was an invention of smugglers who needed to frighten prying eyes away from the bay on the nights they landed their cargo. Other characters which contribute to Jersey legend are the dragon of St Lawrence which tormented villagers and La Pouquelaye, the fairy stone which gave its name to the mischievous 'Puck'.

Some islanders are still superstitious. Legend has it that cattle go down on bended knees on Christmas Eve and anyone who witnesses the animals worshipping will die before the year is out. Several of the old farmers still make sure their cattle are bedded well before the midnight hour.

Among Jersey's strange customs is *les visites du branchage*, a twice-yearly inspection by the parish Constable, Centeniers, Vingteniers, Road Committee and Road Inspectors to see that overhanging branches are not encroaching on roads and footpaths.

Battle of Flowers creation

Morris Men

Festivals

Jersey hosts various festivals throughout the year, the most celebrated of which is the **Battle of Flowers** held on the second Thursday in August. Attracting thousands of visitors, the parade features spectacular floats decorated with flowers and accompanied by marching bands, beauty queens headed by Miss Jersey and a celebrity Mr Battle. On the Friday evening selected floats and bands take part in the **Illuminated Moonlight Parade**. Flower, food and music festivals are hosted throughout the year (apply to Jersey Tourism for dates which change annually). Major festivities are taking place all over the island in 2004, celebrating 800 years of allegiance to the British crown. From 25–27 June Mont Orgueil Castle will be transformed into a medieval market place, soldiers will reenact battles, jousters will perform and medieval ships will be anchored in Gorey port.

Literature and the Arts

Lillie Langtry

Several famous literary and artistic figures have strong Jersey connections. The island's most famous painter was John Everett Millais (1829–96), a founder member of the Pre-Raphaelite brotherhood, who later became a fashionable painter of portraits, costume history and genre pieces. His painting of Lillie Langtry can be seen in the Jersey Museum (*see Route 1, page 19*). The great French writer and political activist, Victor Hugo (1802–85), spent three years in Jersey following his exile from France in 1851. Modern-day Jersey attracts a different style of novelist. The most famous author is Jack Higgins (Harry Patterson), author of *The Eagle Has Landed.*

Venues for theatre, music and the arts

In St Helier, the Jersey Arts Centre, Phillips Street (tel: 01534 700444) hosts plays, concerts and exhibitions of local and national artists. Fort Regent's Gloucester Hall (tel: 01534 500200) can be transformed from a sports hall into a 2,000-seat auditorium for concerts and shows. The restored Opera House in Gloucester Street (tel: 01534 511115) hosts theatrical, musical and operatic productions. Its was built in 1900 on the site of the Theatre Royal, destroyed by fire the year before. Lillie Langtry, who took up acting in 1881, performed here on its opening night.

The Opera House

The Jersey Museum in St Helier has a gallery of 19th-century paintings of Jersey and hosts exhibitions of living local artists. In Trinity, the Jersey Heritage Trust Sir Francis Cook Gallery, Route de Trinité, is open only during temporary exhibitions when visitors can also see the permanent collection of works by the late Sir Francis Cook.

Food and Drink

Opposite: oysters are now mostly farmed

Jersey has two culinary claims to fame: the uniquely flavoured Jersey royal potato and the rich, creamy milk from the Jersey cow. The delicious potatoes, which were first propagated in 1880, are ready for digging as early as April – well before the earliest new potatoes in the UK. Many are grown for export to the UK, but, for those who happen to be in Jersey in spring, there is nothing to compare with a new Jersey Royal straight from the soil.

For the islanders fishing has always been a way of life. In the Middle Ages the abundance of conger, which was salted, dried and shipped to England, led to the nickname 'Isle of the Congers', and from the 17th century, fortunes were made from the cod banks of Newfoundland. Boats still go out to lay the lobster pots and fish for bream, bass, cod, conger, monkfish, grey mullet and mackerel, but the shores have been overfished and species such as the indigenous ormer, prized for its unique flavour and mother-of-pearl shell, is becoming a gourmet rarity. Among the locally caught seafood featuring on menus are lobster, scallops, chancre and spider crabs, clams and shrimps. Mussels and prawns are imported, and oysters, which used to thrive along the shores of the east coast, are now successfully farmed.

Fisherman's catch at Bonne Nuit

65

In the past the basic ingredients of many traditional Jersey dishes were dried red and white beans, formerly grown on every farm on the island. The Jersey Bean Crock, said to be the origin of baked beans, is a variation of the French cassoulet, comprising five different kinds of dried beans, pigs' trotter, belly of pork or shin of beef, carrot and onion. Nowadays the dish is rarely made, but Jersey beans are making a comeback.

The unapppetisingly-named Jersey 'black butter' is in fact a type of apple preserve. This used to be produced in vast quanties every autumn, a typical recipe comprising 700lb of apples, 10 gallons of cider, 20lb of sugar, 24 lemons and 3lb of spices. Cooking carried on all day and night, with family members stirring the huge pot and making merry with song and dance. The hot sticky mixture was then stored in jars, to last until the following autumn. The centuries-old tradition is kept alive by the Jersey Young Farmers Club who hold black butter nights in November and a few other enthusiasts who make it in smaller quantities. Among other Jersey specialities are conger eel soup, made with the head of the eel boiled in milk and garnished with marigold flower petals, *Des bourdélots*, apples baked in pastry, *des Mèrvelles* or Jersey Wonders, doughnut-like cakes, traditionally cooked as the tide went out, and cabbage loaf – crusty white bread baked in large cabbage leaves, and still sold in some bakeries.

Traditional produce at Hamptonne Country Life Museum

The humble prawn sandwich

Restaurant at Samarès Manor

Cider used to be the drink of the island and large quantities were exported from the mid-17th century to the mid-19th century. One of the few places where it is made today is La Mare Vineyards, St Mary, which also produces Jersey's only wines (*see Route 3, page 36*).

Restaurants

Jersey has around 200 restaurants, including a handful which might pass muster in London. The island tries hard to promote its food, each May hosting a Good Food Festival, when restaurant celebrities from around the world join Jersey's top chefs to show off the best of the island's produce. Retired tax-exiles and prosperous resident financiers and lawyers ensure a year-round clientèle for the best restaurants and even the discerning French come across the Channel on day trips to indulge their palates.

Cream tea at Jersey Pottery

Jersey's capital, St Helier, has a surprising dearth of gourmet restaurants and the best places tend to be scattered around the island, mostly on the coast. At the lower end of the scale, there's no shortage of places serving fast food and snacks. Most beaches have at least one café, some serving seafood, crab sandwiches, home-made cakes and cream teas. The latter can vary from the pre-packed variety to freshly made scones with lashings of thick Jersey cream and strawberry jam.

The *Jersey Eating Out Guide* (available at nominal cost from Jersey Tourism in Liberation Square, St Helier) is a useful booklet giving details of recommended restaurants, cafés and pubs on the island.

The restaurants in this selection are listed according to the following price categories: £££ = expensive (over £55 for two); ££ = moderate (£30–55 for two); £ = Inexpensive (under £30 for two). Price brackets include house wine.

Gorey

Jersey Pottery Restaurant, Gorey Village, Grouville, tel: 01534 851119. A favourite among islanders for excellent value seafood and delightful garden setting. (Cheaper fare is served in the Spinnaker Grill, a self-service restaurant with cheerful nautical decor.) Pottery production takes place on the premises (*see page 48*). ££–£££.

Ming's Dynasty, Gorey Pier, tel: 01534 856886. Chinese dining with views of the harbour. Try duck or shark's fin soup, fresh fillet of sole Cantonese or sizzling beef. Takeaways available. £–££.

Secret Garden, Gorey Common, Grouville, tel: 01534 85299. Appropriately named, within a delightful walled garden. Famous for cream teas and gâteaux, it also serves home-made pies, salads, and fresh fish and seafood. £.

Suma's, Gorey Hill, Gorey, tel: 01534 853291. Fresh, innovative cuisine in a stylish restaurant overlooking Gorey harbour and castle. English cuisine with Mediterranean and Oriental overtones. Good value set lunches – reserve a table al fresco. ££–£££.

The Village Bistro, Gorey Village, Grouville, tel: 01534 853429. One of only two restaurants in Jersey which have a Michelin star. Imaginative dishes at affordable prices. ££.

Grouville

Borsalino Rocque, La Grande Route des Sablons, Grouville, tel: 01534 852111. Known for its seafood. Book in advance for a table in the floral conservatory. Music from 11pm. ££–£££.

Rozel

Château La Chaire, Rozel Bay, St Martin, tel: 01534 863354. Part of the Château La Chaire Hotel, offering the best cuisine on the north coast. £££.

Mimosa Café and Restaurant. La Brecque du Nord, Rozel, Trinity, tel: 01534 864713. Generous cream teas, lunches and seafood specials. Take-aways available. £.

St Aubin

Blue Fish 2, La Neuve Route, St Aubin, tel: 01534 747118. Popular fish restaurant set back from the main road through St Aubin. Relaxed atmosphere, nautical decor, modern cuisine. Reservations advised, especially for outdoor tables in summer. ££.

La Barca, Bulwarks, St Aubin, tel: 01534 44275. Cheerful Italian trattoria by the harbour. ££.

Old Court House Inn, St Aubin, St Brelade, tel: 01534 46433. Historic harbour-side house, converted into a hotel. Meals are served in the conservatory or the upstairs restaurant. Specialities are lobster, gambas and crab. £££.

Fresh fish

The best fish and chips in town

Jersey Museum M 🚶

St Brelade

Hotel l'Horizon, St Brelade's Bay, tel: 01534 743101. The Crystal Room and the Grill offer bay views and some of the best cuisine on the island. The Brasserie within the leisure centre serves light meals. ££ (Brasserie) £££ (Crystal Room, Grill).

Jambo, St Brelade's Bay, tel: 01534 45801 Chinese, bay-view restaurant, specialising in Peking and Szechuan dishes. ££.

Pizza Express, St Brelade's Bay, tel: 01534 499049. Excellent pizzas from well-known UK chain. Award-winning glass building with fine views of the bay. £.

St Clement

Green Island Restaurant, Green Island, St Clement, tel: 01534 857787. Facing Green Island. Excellent value seafood and fish including char-grilled scallops, sand eels and sea bass. ££.

St Helier

Albert Ramsbottom, 90–92 Halkett Place, St Helier, tel: 01534 721395. The best fish and chips in town. Huge portions and very friendly. £.

Bistrot du Chambertin, 20 Beresford Street, tel: 01534 759032. Good value, authentic French cuisine in attractive setting. ££.

Bistro Central, 7–11 Don Street, St Helier, tel: 01534 876933. French-style bistro, in the heart of St Helier. Specialities are fish and shell fish. £££.

Café des Artistes, King Street, St Helier, tel: 01534 639990. Café and brasserie within Voisins department store in the centre of St Helier. £.

La Capannina, 65–67 Halkett Place, St Helier, tel: 01534 34602. Smart Italian restaurant, popular with businessmen at lunchtime £££.

City Restaurant and Bar, 75–77 Halkett Place, tel: 01534 510096. Contemporary café, with internet facilities (free access with a meal). £–££.

La Mangeoire, Central Market, tel: 01534 724609. Tempting French gâteaux and pastries by the fountain in the food market. £.

The Museum Brasserie, Jersey Museum, Weighbrdge, St Helier, tel: 01534 510069. International cuisine. Choose from set menus or simple á la carte menus. Open all day for coffee and cakes. £–££.

The Olive Branch, 39 Colomberie, St Helier, tel: 01534 615993. Stylish place for pizzas, cooked in wood-filled oven. Good pasta too. £–££.

Victoria's, Grand Hotel, Esplanade, St Helier, tel: 01534 872255. A plush hotel restaurant, overlooking St Helier's waterfront. Save this one for a special occasion. £££.

St Martin

Frère de Mer, Rozel Hill, St Martin, tel: 01534 861000. Good value seafood restaurant with superb views across to France from the terrace. ££.

St Ouen's Bay

El Tico, Five Mile Road, St Ouen, tel: 01534 482649. Beach café with good sandwiches and home-made cakes and pies. The terrace offers excellent views of the surfers. £.

St Peter

The Carvery, Les Charrières Hotel, St Peter, tel: 01534 481480. Very popular for Sunday roast lunch. Dinner only Monday to Saturday. ££.

St Saviour

Longueville Manor, Longueville Road, St Saviour, tel: 01534 25501. Long-established, award-winning restaurant serving gourmet cuisine in oak-panelled dining room. Seasonal produce from the kitchen garden. Vegetarian and children's menus available. £££.

Pubs

Grève de Lecq

Moulin de Lecq, Grève de Lecq, tel: 482818. 14th-century inn, with a working water mill. Barbecue, fish dishes and snacks. Particularly good for families, as it has a play area. £.

Moulin de Lecq

Ouaisné Bay

Old Smugglers' Inn, Ouaisné Bay, tel: 741510. Very popular pub, originally 17th-century cottages. Good choice of food from sandwiches and snacks to chicken satay and seafood ragout.

Portelet Bay

Old Portelet Inn, Portelet Bay, tel: 01534 741899. Converted farmhouse in a scenic spot above the bay. Standard pub grub. Live entertainment most nights.

Rozel Bay

Rozel Bay Inn, Rozel Bay, St Martin, tel: 01534 863438. Some of the best pub food on the island, including lobster, crabs and seafood platter. Food served in upstairs restaurant or pub below.

St Peter's Village

The Star & Tipsy Toad, St Peter's village, St Peter, tel: 01534 485556. Home-brewed ales such as Tipsy Toad or Horny Toad. Brewery tours and tastings by prior arrangement.

Old Smugglers' Inn

Cycling

See page 57 for cycling on Jersey. There are plenty of places to hire bikes. Delivery is normally free to St Helier hotels; elsewhere there's a small delivery charge. In St Helier, try Aardvark & Zebra Cycles, 8–9 Esplanade, tel: 01534 736556, near the tourist office.

Cycling options

Walking

See pages 52–56

Horse riding

Several stables offer tuition and rides, though beach rides are only available to experienced riders. Le Claire Riding & Livery Stables at La Rue Militaire, St John, offers scenic country hacks. Tel: 01534 862823.

Golf

To play at the Royal Jersey Golf Club at Grouville, tel: 01534 854416, or La Moye at St Brelade, tel: 01534 747166, both 18-hole, you need to be a member of a recognised golf club. Others can play at Les Mielles Golf and Country Club, St Ouen's Bay, tel: 01534 482787, Wheatlands, St Peter, tel: 01534 888844, Les Ormes, St Brelade, tel: 01534 497000, and Jersey Recreation Grounds, Grève d'Azette, St Clement, tel: 01534 721938.

Golf at Grouville

Tennis

The Caesarean Tennis Club at Grands Vaux has courts to hire for non-members, but players are expected to wear proper tennis clothes. Tel: 01534 89321. Courts are also available at the Jersey Recreation Grounds at Grève d'Azette, St Clement, tel: 01534 721938, the Quennevais Sports Centre, St Brelade, tel: 01534 490909, and there are indoor courts at Les Ormes, St Brelade, tel: 01534 497000.

Boat trips

Cruiser trips along the south coast depart from Albert Quay, St Helier. Reservations should be made at hotel receptions or at the kiosk next to the marina.

Fishing

Wrasse, bass, grey mullet, black bream, pollack, garfish, mackerel and conger eel are all caught offshore. For boat fishing trips from St Helier, contact David Nuth, tel: 01534 858046 or 7797 728 316. The piers on the north coast are popular for rod fishing. Low tide is the best time for finding prawns, crabs and small fish in the rock pools. In St Aubin during spring tides razor fish can be enticed from the sands by sprinkling salt on their key-shaped holes. For fly fishing, day tickets are available for the reservoirs of Val de la Mare, Grands Vaux and Queen's Valley, all of which are stocked with trout. Full details are available from the fishing tackle shop in St Helier market.

Diving

The Jersey sea is clean, visibility is good and marine life plentiful. The Jersey Diving School at Bouley Bay is a five-star diving centre which welcomes divers of all standards, including beginners. Tel: 01534 866990. More experienced divers can visit the wrecks of ships which sank during World War II and others which have been deliberately scuttled to provide shelter for marine life.

Leisure and Fitness

The new Waterfront Centre at St Helier features a fitness club and the Aqua Centre, tel: 01534 734524. Leisure and outdoor pools, with sundeck and diving area. Fort Regent, tel: 01534 500200, offers over 23 acres (9 hectares) of fun and sport from billiards and bowling to squash and swimming.

Sailing

The waters around the Channel Islands are popular for yachting but the sunken reefs, big tides and strong currents make it unsuitable for inexperienced sailors. Boats can be chartered for those with experience, alternatively skippers can be hired. St Helier makes a good base for circular and day cruises. Information from the St Helier Yacht Club, South Pier, tel: 01534 721307.

Surfing at St Ouen's

Surfing and windsurfing

St Ouen's Bay has excellent surf and is the venue for international surfing competitions in summer. Inexperienced surfers should always keep to the areas between flags, which are surveyed by lifeguards. Several companies along the bay hire out surf equipment and offer tuition, including the Jersey Surfing School at the Watersplash, tel: 01534 484005.

St Aubin's Bay, St Brelade's Bay, Grouville and St Ouen's Bay are the most popular for windsurfing.

Other watersports

Waterskiing, water boarding, speed boat and banana rides are available at St Brelade's Bay, St Aubin (La Haule slipway) and at the Gorey watersports Centre, Grouville. Jet skis and waterboarding are also available at St Aubin and self-drive glass-bottom boats at Grouville.

Workout at Fort Regent

Getting There

Opposite: shades of St Helier

Package holidays to Jersey, either by sea or air, can be arranged through British tour operators. Alternatively, most of the hotels, guest houses and self-catering establishments on the island can arrange travel for you, as well as travel insurance and car rental.

For those travelling independently, flight details are available from any travel agent in the UK or from Jersey specialists such as Channel Island Travel Services (tel: 01534 496600; www.jerseytravel.com) who can take care of flights from UK airports, sea travel or car hire.

By air

Direct flights operate to Jersey from over 25 UK airports and several major European airports. The three main airlines operating services to Jersey from the UK are British Airways (tel: 0870 8509850; www.ba.com), British European Airways (tel: 0871 7000123; www.flybe.com and bmibaby (tel: 0870 2642229; www.bmibaby.com). Prices vary hugely and it's worth shopping around for low cost flights. Considerable savings can be made by booking online. Aurigny Air Services (tel: 01481 822886) fly from Southampton and provide a Channel Island hopping service between Jersey, Alderney and Guernsey.

Taxis are available at Jersey airport and in season a bus leaves every 15 minutes for St Helier.

Flying Jersey European

By sea

Condor Ferries (tel: 0845 3452000; www.condorferries. co.uk) operate a high-speed catamaran service to Jersey. In winter it runs from Weymouth only; from April to October there are regular crossings from Weymouth and Poole. The futuristic-looking 'Wavepiercer', which takes cars as well as passengers, travels at 40mph and the crossing time to Jersey is around 3 hours if you go to Jersey direct, slightly longer if you go via Guernsey. Bad weather conditions can lead to the cancellation of the crossing.

Condor also operates a traditional ferry (Mon–Sat all year) which takes 10 hours to Jersey from Portsmouth. From Jersey you can take day trips to Brittany, Guernsey, Sark and Herm. Emeraude Lines (tel: 01534 766566; www.emeraude.co.uk) operate a high-speed car ferry service between St Malo and Jersey (2hrs 30 mins).

St Helier ferry port

Inter-island ferries

Condor Ferries (tel: 0845 3452000) operate day trips and short breaks to St Malo and day trips to Guernsey, with connections on to Sark and Herm. A passport is required for trips to France.

Car hire

Car hire prices in the Channel Islands are among the cheapest in Europe, and the price of fuel is much lower than in the UK. Visitors hiring cars must produce a valid driving licence and be aged 21 and over. Car hire companies are abundant and competitive. Ideal Hire Cars offer some of the cheapest rates, both for new and second-hand (but reliable) cars.

Car hire companies include: Avis, St Peter, tel: 01534 519100; www.avisjersey.co.uk; Europcar, La Moye, St Brelade, tel: 01534 747770; www: europcarjersey.com Hertz, Jersey Airport, tel: 01534 636666; www.jerseyservices com/hertz; and Zebra Hire, 9 Esplanade, St Helier, tel: 01534 736556; www.zebrahire.com

Buses

Connex Transport Jersey Ltd, tel: 01534 721201, provides a network of buses from the central bus station at Weighbridge, St Helier. The new Easylink is a hop-on hop-off service linking St Helier with the west and east coasts and the most popular attractions on the island. Explorer tickets for both services are available from the bus station.

Cycling

See pages 57 and 70

Driving

The island's maximum speed-limit is 40mph, reduced to 30mph or 20mph in some town areas and to 15mph on Green Lanes (*see page 52*). In the event of an accident, call the police on 612612 or, in an emergency, 999.

Parking

In St Helier the easiest option is to park in one of the five multi-storey car parks. Parking cards (or 'scratchcards'), which must be displayed, are available from garages and many shops, but *not* in the car parks themselves. The cards are also used in a few other busy areas, but parking elsewhere is usually free. Some free parking, however, is controlled by parking discs, provided by car-hire companies or obtainable from the Town Hall and Jersey Tourism.

Le Petit Train

Small trains with guided commentaries operate from St Helier. One does a half-hour tour of the town, departing from the top of Queen Street Precinct, and the two others skirt the bay to St Aubin, starting opposite the Grand Hotel. Evening trips operate in summer.

74

St Helier's esplanade train

Facts for the Visitor

Travel documents

No passport is required for visitors travelling from the British Isles and the Republic of Ireland. Some airlines now require photographic ID in order to travel

Tourist information

The Jersey Tourism Visitor Services Centre in Liberation Square, St Helier, has a wealth of information on the island and can arrange accommodation. It is open daily from May–Sept, and off-season Mon–Fri 8.30am– 5.30pm, Sat 9am–1pm, tel: 01534 500700. Most of the information can be accessed on its website, www.jersey.com

Sightseeing

Most attractions are free for young children and substantial reductions are given to Senior Citizens and students.

Young children usually go free

Banks

Although Jersey has its own currency, in the same denominations as UK notes and coins, British money is freely accepted on the island, as are most credit cards and UK cheques supported by a banker's card. Some shops now accept euros.

Post offices

The main post office is located in Broad Street, St Helier and is open Mon–Fri 8.30am–5pm, Sat 9am– 2pm. Jersey postage stamps, available from post offices and some shops, must be used on all mail.

Telephone and internet

Public call boxes have mainly card phones, which also take credit cards. Jersey Phonecards are available from post offices, newsagents and garages. The area code for Jersey from the UK is 01534, STD codes for the UK from Jersey are the same as those used from the UK. 'Pay as you Go' phones rarely function in Jersey and certain mobile networks require a roaming facility. Internet Access is available at Jersey Library, Halkett Place, St Helier, tel: 01534 759991, and at All-Type Business Centre, Royal Square, St Helier, tel: 01534 724100.

Card phones

Time

The Channel Islands follow Greenwich Mean Time (GMT).

Opening times

Bank, shop and post office opening times are the same as in the UK. Most of the museums and tourist attractions are open Apr–Oct 9am or 10am to 5pm.

Public holidays

These are the same as those of the UK with the addition of Liberation Day on 9 May.

Downtown St Helier

Shopping

The chief attraction of shopping in Jersey is the duty and VAT-free goods. However, this is not apparent in many shops which put up prices for 'shipping costs'. The main centre is St Helier, with its pedestrianised shopping streets and food and fish market. The shops are similar to those you would find on a UK high street, but with a notable abundance of cosmetics. Several craft centres are dotted around the island, Jersey Pottery (*see page 48*) being the most famous.

Nightlife

Nightlife is mainly confined to St Helier and consists of pubs and discos primarily aimed at young residents and tourists. The *Jersey Evening Post* is the best place to find out about performances by live bands, jazz concerts, DJs, etc. A new focus of nightlife is the Waterfront Centre in St Helier, whose attractions include the Liquid Nightclub, Chicago Rock Café, bars and fast food outlets. The new 10-screen Cineworld (tel: 0871 220800) is the first UK cinema to offer VIP boxes (complete with waitress service). Pubs are open on weekdays 9am–11pm, Sun 11am–11pm.

Health and medical services

Visitors requiring medical attention should call: 01534 616883 Mon–Fri 8.30am–4.30pm to be connected to a GP surgery who will issue an appointment and the location of the surgery for that day. There is no charge for visitors from the UK and other countries with a reciprocal agreement. Out of hours, call the General Hospital in St Helier which has a 24 hour emergency unit, tel: 01534 622000.

Emergencies

In an emergency, dial 999 for police, fire, ambulance or sea rescue.

Disabled access

An access guide for disabled visitors can be obtained from Jersey Tourism or downloaded from their website (*see page 75*). Special parking areas are available for Orange and Blue Badge holders. Public conveniences for the disabled, fitted with radar locks, can be found in all the main centres and at most of the beaches. Jersey Tourism also publishes a list of companies that can provide special equipment for the disabled.

Jersey for Children

With its sandy beaches, clean seas and rock pools, Jersey is ideal for children. Most of the museums and attractions on the island are geared to all ages, particularly the Maritime Museum (*see page 15*), Samarès Manor and Living Legend (*see page 49*). Another favourite is **Elizabeth Castle** (*see page 20*), especially the journey across to the islet in the amphibian ferry.

Nature enthusiasts will enjoy the exotic butterflies which breed among tropical flora at the **Butterfly Centre**, Haute Tombette at St Mary; and the farmyard animals at **Hamptonne Country Life Museum** (*see page 35*). The **Amaizin Maze** (La Houge Farm, La Grande Route de St Pierre, St Peter, tel: 01534 482116) is constructed entirely of maize, and provides fun for all ages. Art and craft enthusiasts will enjoy Glaze Craze at Jersey Pottery (*see page 48)*, where you can paint and decorate a plain mug, plate or pig and have it glazed by the pottery.

At **Treasures of the Earth** (daily 9.30am–5pm), on La Route de l'Etacq, St Ouen, a journey through caverns, grottos and 'The Magic Temple' reveals glowing crystallised minerals, gemstones, fossils and prehistoric creatures.

Young children will be quite content to spend the day messing around in rock pools, fishing for shrimps, crabs and devil fish. Every beach shop is well equipped with cheap nets and buckets. The best beaches for swimming are St Brelade's and St Aubin's where the sand shelves gently and the waters are normally calm. However, older children who are good swimmers will love body surfing on the waves at St Ouen's. Boogy boards are available for hire at various points.

The island has several parks and gardens, many with play areas for children. **Coronation Park** at Millbrook is one of the most popular for children. **Sunset Flower Centre**, behind St Ouen's Bay, has a tropical bird garden with macaws and cockatoos, and a pond stocked with massive trout which feed on pellets sold on the premises.

Jersey's answer to a wet day is **Fort Regent** in St Helier (daily 10am–5pm, tel: 01534 500200). This huge leisure complex has sufficient attractions to keep children amused for days. The entrance charge covers all the entertainment and tourist attractions, including an aquarium, vivarium, play areas for young children, exhibitions, swimming, live entertainment, shows in high season and a swim in the pool. The extensive recreation and sports facilities (*see page 15*) include a skate park, funfair rides, Quasar (laser guns), crazy golf, trampolining and a toddlers' gym. The Aqua Centre on St Helier's new waterfront provides a leisure pool with wave machine and outdoor pool with flumes.

Butterfly Centre

Beach pursuits

A new friend

St Helier's Royal Yacht Hotel

Accommodation

La Bonne Vie

The Grand

Jersey has more than 500 registered hotels and guest houses, but very little self-catering accommodation. Prices for accommodation range from the reasonable to the ridiculous, so there is somewhere for everyone. Bookings can be made through Jersey Tourism, tel: 01534 500888, or online at: www.jerseyhols.com For a copy of the accommodation brochure call: 01534 500800 or download a copy from the Jersey Tourism website, www.jersey.com

Hotel selection

The selection below is listed acording to the following categories: **££££** (over £150 per night double); **£££** (£110–150); **££** (£70–110); **£** (under £70).

St Helier

La Bonne Vie, Roseville St, tel: 01534 735955. This ia a charming Victorian guest house close to the beach and with a pool. **£**.

The Grand, The Esplanade, tel: 01543 722301: www.devereonline.co.uk Overlooking St Aubin's Bay, the hotel lives up to its name and is noted for cuisine. **£££**.

Hotel de France, St Saviour's Road, tel: 01534 614000; www.defrance.co.uk Elegant and comfortable. Numerous facilities include pools, cinema and health centre. **£££**.

Millbrook House, Rue de Trachy, Millbrook, tel: 01534 733036; www.millbrookhousehotel.com Delightful country house hotel, converted from a restored 18th-century residence, set in 10 acres (4 hectares) of park and gardens. **££**.

Uplands, St John's Road, Mont à l'Abbe tel: 01534 873006; www.morvanhotels.com A family-run hotel, based around a set of old granite buildings and located in its own farmland. **££**.

Bouley Bay
Water's Edge Hotel, Bouley Bay, Trinity, tel: 01534 862777; www.watersedgehotel.co.je Above pebble beach, with beautiful views. ££.

Gorey
Old Court House Hotel, Gorey Village, Grouville, tel: 01534 854444; www.ochhotel.co.uk Popular family hotel on the edge of Gorey. ££.
Moorings Hotel, **Gorey Pier**, tel: 01534 853633; www. themooringshotel.com Small, exclusive hotel at the foot of Mont Orgueil, noted for cuisine, especially seafood. 16 rooms only. ££–£££.

Rozel
Chateau La Chaire, Rozel Bay, St Martin, tel: 01534 863354; www.chateau-la-chaire.co.uk Smart, country house hotel, at the foot of Rozel Valley. Well known for cuisine (*see page 67*). £££.

St Aubin
Harbour View, St Aubin Harbour, tel: 01534 741585; www.harbourview.je Charming guest house with garden bistro. 13 rooms. £.
Old Court House Inn, St Aubin Harbour, tel: 01534 746433; www.oldcourthousejersey.com Fine harbourview building dating back to 1450. *See page 68* for restaurant. ££–£££.

Old Court House Inn

St Brelade's Bay
Atlantic Hotel, La Moye, St Brelade, tel: 01534 744101; www.theatlantichotel.com Magnificent views over St Ouen's Bay. Health and leisure centre, indoor and outdoor pools, sauna, tennis courts. ££££.
Golden Sands, St Brelade's Bay, tel: 01534 741241. Modern hotel, well-situated with steps down to the beach. ££.
L'Horizon, St Brelade's Bay, tel: 01534 743101; www.handpicked.co/uk/l'horizon Exceptionally comfortable and civilised, overlooking bay. ££££.
St Brelade's Bay Hotel, St Brelade's Bay, tel: 01534 746141; www.stbreladesbayhotel.com Elegant hotel in seven acres of gardens, across the road from St Brelade's Beach. ££££.

St Brelade's Bay Hotel

St Saviour
Champ Colin, Route du Champ Colin, tel: 01534 851877. Peaceful, rural guest house. £.
Longueville Manor, St Saviour, tel: 01534 725501; www.longuevillemanor.com Exclusive country-house hotel in 15 acres (6 hectares) of grounds. Elegant rooms, paintings and antiques. ££££.

Index